Living with Genetic Syndromes
Associated with Intellectual Disability

Living with Genetic Syndromes Associated with Intellectual Disability

Marga Hogenboom

Jessica Kingsley Publishers
London and Philadelphia

The right of Marga Hogenboom to be identified as author of this work has been asserted by her in accordance with the Copyright, Designs and Patents Act 1988.

First published in the United Kingdom in 2001 by
Jessica Kingsley Publishers Ltd
116 Pentonville Road,
London N1 9JB, England
and
325 Chestnut Street,
Philadelphia, PA 19106, USA.

Copyright © 2001 Marga Hogenboom

Library of Congress Cataloging in Publication Data
A CIP record for this book is available from the Library of Congress

British Library Cataloguing in Publication Data
A CIP record for this book is available from the British Library

ISBN 1 85302 984 X ✓

Printed and Bound in Great Britain by
Athenaeum Press, Gateshead, Tyne and Wear

I dedicate this book to Casper Hauser,
Child of Europe

Contents

Acknowledgements

It has been a joy to find help when I was looking for it. Many people have given their support to this project. Theresa McCafferty helped me to kick-start the writing process. We studied the different syndromes in the therapy college in Camphill schools for two years and this helped me further with the understanding of all these conditions. Mario Domen has done an enormous amount of typing and editing, and he kept me going during the initial phase of the project. Without him I would never have dared to start this book. The circle widened; Eileen Billett helped with the typing, John Anderson and Sandra Stoddard corrected the English and Max Desorgher used his editing skills to make it presentable.

Quite a few people read the script and made comments – Dr Martin Niemeyer, Professor Bremer, Jaap van der Wal, Dr Anneke Meuwese and Jackie Waters.

Most importantly, my gratitude goes to the people whose lives I have shared and described. My ultimate aim was to respect both their dignity and the dignity of anyone with a genetic syndrome. Genes and chromosomes can never explain their humanity. All the people whose life stories I told or their parents gave permission for me to do so and were delighted by the special interest I showed in them. Only Alistair, in the chapter on Williams Syndrome, could not do so because he has passed away. His mother supported his inclusion in the book before her death. I would also like to thank my father (who died some years ago) and my mother; without them I wouldn't be here.

Who would ever have thought when I started this that so many people would be involved in the project?

I have done my best to ensure that the factual information is up-to-date and accurate, but any mistakes are my own responsibility. Sometimes I doubted my ability to write a book about syndromes when there are many people who are more knowledgeable and experienced in working with these syndromes. I must emphasize that it is written out of my own experience as a doctor and the people I describe are youngsters who live in a residential school, in a Camphill place. So maybe some aspects of my experiences can't be generalized to other people who are in different circumstances. I still hope that this book will be helpful to people with genetic syndromes, parents and carers. I would be very interested in any responses, corrections or other comments regarding this book.

CHAPTER ONE

Introduction

Whenever I visit the hospital in Aberdeen where I often go to continue my studies, I like to walk through the medical faculty and take a look at all the young medical students there; a feeling of nostalgia arises in me with memories of my own student days. It seems long ago that I was a student in Utrecht, a university town in the middle of Holland with a distinguished past reaching back to the seventeenth century. Utrecht is a charming old city with a majestic cathedral, small streets and canals which were used to transport goods by boat and barge in former days, lined on both sides with warehouses. Many of these warehouses have now been transformed into cafés, which have become an important part of student life. The medical school used to be housed in various buildings throughout the town and I remember how we used to race our bikes through the inner city streets between lectures with a microscope strapped onto the luggage carrier. The oldest faculty building housed the anatomical laboratory, and before entering the lecture hall you could walk through the museum, which was full of anatomical curiosities stored in bottles of alcohol. It gave the whole atmosphere a slightly unusual colour.

When I was in my fourth year, a commotion arose amongst us students; a new professor of psychiatry was appointed, Herman Meir van Praag. He was well known for his interest in biological psychiatry – in researching the biochemical processes in the brain and their relationship to psychiatric behaviour. There was a vague feeling of disapproval amongst us. This was the time of the anti-psychiatry movement; the origins of disturbed behaviour were being sought in pathological interactions with the environment and with family dynamics. Just recently I discovered that there had been quite a controversy around Herman van Praag. In 1997 I read an article about him entitled 'Life of Struggle' (van Bos 1997). Herman van Praag recalled those years in Utrecht: it seems that the resistance against his work was quite outspoken and life wasn't easy for him. His children even needed occasional police protection on their way to school. But Herman van Praag had already experienced struggle in his teenage years – he was Jewish, and he and his family had been interned in a camp during the Second World War, only just surviving the ordeal.

Twenty years later, I find myself working as a doctor in a medical practice connected with a school for children with special needs. It is a residential school although the children are only here during term times. The children live with carers in an extended family setting. The carers and their families share the life of the pupils in a full and rewarding life. There is a great diversity of pupils – from the teenager with behaviour problems to the withdrawn, non-speaking, non-toilet-trained child with autism. A large percentage of our pupils have genetic disorders and my interest is in the impact this has on the children. How is it possible that children with common chromosomal disorders such as Down or Prader-Willi Syndromes have so much in common, not just in outward appearance but also in habits, behaviours or manners of speaking?

One day I was looking through a medical textbook on genetics and I became engrossed. I recognized one of our pupils, Mira, in the description of a certain syndrome. The book described it as a rare syndrome with 47 chromosomes instead of 46. The extra chromosome is number 15, the so-called 15q-Marker Syndrome. I could recognize her in the description: she grows slowly and I sometimes wondered about the medical reason for this. She also has epilepsy. She seems to be autistic, but as I tried to explain to her mother, her autism has a different quality from that of most autistic children. Typically, she won't look at us, but gazes upwards, above us, as a newborn baby would do. She cannot cope with change and can often be found playing, fairy-like, with leaves or jumping through the house singing in her own language. Both these aspects were clearly there in the syndrome described in the article.

When my first enthusiasm had ebbed a little, many questions came to me. Can a human being be explained through her chromosomes? Can I understand a human being better through her chromosomes? How would this change my relationship to 'biological psychiatry'? Where was Mira in all of this – the Mira who loves it when people make music, who adores her musical father, who has a close connection to her mother and her Japanese carer, who moved with Mira when she was placed in a different house community, or Mira the young pure being who can look so enchanting with beautiful plaited hair, or Mira who can become distressed when she gets so high that she cannot stop running, speaking in her own singsong language? To know that much of this is due to her syndrome can give a certain acceptance, an inner peace: the girl behind the syndrome becomes visible. Many aspects are genetically determined, such as her small stature and the peculiar behaviour; but her biography is unique. Through her biography her individuality shines through.

There is a second reason why I felt compelled to write this book; it has to do with my own (genetic?) background. My father was a genetic engineer. He did it the old-fashioned way: not in laboratories but with fields of corn. In 1947 he crossed a corn which was cold-resistant but did not grow very well, with an American variety which ripened late. The result was a corn variety which was suitable for the Dutch climate and became the basis of West European corn culture.

He had a keen interest in the colour of eyes. 'If you have brown eyes and your mother's are blue, I am sure that your father had brown eyes.' This was often his opening remark when he met somebody. My future husband was greeted in this way. My father felt at home with Mendel's laws of heredity. It amused me, but the difficulty started when my behaviour was approached in the same way, that certain characteristics were supposed to have been inherited from my old auntie Kee and old auntie Koo. This annoyed me and I felt like getting cross and saying 'but I am different'; however, I was well educated and held my tongue.

This book is an attempt to find an answer to these questions: What is determined by our genes? And where is our freedom?

CHAPTER TWO

An Oasis of Humanity

One Saturday in January, the sun is shining in a clear blue sky with some grey clouds. My children are playing happily as I make my way to Dr König's old study to work on my book. Karl König was an Austrian physician of Jewish descent who was forced to flee from the Nazis in 1939. He settled in Scotland and a group of young friends followed him. They were refugees in a strange country while the war raged in Central Europe. This group set itself the task of caring for another group of 'refugees' from society – people with learning disabilities, at a time, 1940, when there were hardly any schools for children with special needs. They took them in and began a community where everybody lived together. There were no paid positions, no salaries and the hours were long. The first place where this community life began was Camphill House, the same house where I had lived together with eleven children with special needs, nine carers, my husband and our three children.

Nowadays it is taken for granted that every child has a right to an education, but in the early 1950s this was a new approach. The impulse that this group of refugees started has spread around the world, and Camphill is now a worldwide network caring for more than 3000 children and adults with special needs. What were the ideals that Dr König tried to realize and on which he founded this approach? The main ideal was to recognize the unique healthy spirit in each person, whatever their race, sex or 'disability'. He also felt strongly that the child with an intellectual disability needed to go to school, so a formal school was created in the Camphill Community.

Dr König was inspired by the teachings of Rudolf Steiner and so he called the school he started 'Camphill Rudolf Steiner School'. Rudolf Steiner was an Austrian philosopher who lived from 1866 until 1925. He was very active, lectured widely and wrote many books. His philosophy is called 'Anthroposophy', which literally means 'awareness of one's humanity'.

Steiner spoke about 'spiritual science', indicating that his insights can be objectified by anyone who follows a path of spiritual development. Nothing should be 'believed' but every statement tested on its true merits. The main core of Anthroposophy is the idea that human beings are different from animals: we are not simply a 'higher animal', but each of us has a unique individuality. This individuality is eternal and follows a path of development through successive earth lives. There is an important element of freedom in Anthroposophy – our lives are not predestined, rather we have the freedom to choose and recognize what we want. Anthroposophy has Christianity in the broadest sense at its heart.

So what is it like to live without a salary or fixed working hours and to share our lives with special needs children? Is it still possible now in the twenty-first century? Do we need to find new ways of working and living together? These are very relevant questions and not easy to answer. The way of life and work allows an intensity and concentration which have been beneficial for the pupils but it also asks an enormous amount of dedication from the carers. Another aspect is that sometimes the large, well-established Camphill communities can seem isolated from the world around them, like islands. This is becoming less and less the case. Collaboration with the outside world is continually increasing and newer communities are much more integrated into their local environment from the start. So the various Camphill communities are searching for an answer to this question – how is it possible to maintain a space for a private life, while still serving the person with special needs in the twenty-first century? Life is not always idealistic in Camphill: tensions arise, responsibilities pile up, a child runs off or is ill, there are aggressive outbursts from pupils and carers get tired.

But the most precious memories are those when I could feel connected with the 'special' children, not as a doctor or carer but as a fellow human being. Those moments of humanity which this life can provide I carry as a treasure within me. One such is that Saturday when I am working in Dr König's historic library, and I feel transported into a different time, closed off from the world around me. After an hour, my hands are cold, some pages have been written and I don't hear my children. Dusk comes, the evening call of a bird. I walk through the half darkened passage to the stately stairs. It is quiet in the house. I open the heavy door of the music room. Here, in the midst of more books, I find an oasis of humanity. Someone plays the piano, another accompanies on the clarinet. One child, mine, sits quietly next to the piano enjoying the music. The fire is on in another part of the room. Through the high windows the colour play of sunset is visible. A child makes a puzzle, using his mouth as an extra tool. My daughter makes friendship bracelets with some children, others stare dreamily into the fire. Music fills the place. Here everybody just enjoys being, and letting time pass by.

I enter with cold hands, my head full of theories about DNA, syndromes and behaviour. I start to relax and breathe deeply. My gaze moves around the room. Adults are knitting; another child looks longingly at the piano. At least five children here have a chromosome abnormality, a syndrome. My eyes search for them, but what I meet is an oasis of humanity. This image has remained in the background of my mind, allowing me to write this book; it brought the bare facts of medical science and statistics to life. In writing this book, I feel especially inspired by Oliver Sacks, who continued the tradition of 'case studies', where people with illnesses are described in their own context. In his books he is always searching for the personality who lives with the syndrome. He writes:

> If one looks at the charts of patients institutionalised in asylums and state hospitals in the 1920s and 1930s one finds extremely detailed clinical and phenomenological observations, often embedded in narratives of an almost novelistic richness and density. With the institution of rigid diagnostic criteria and

manuals this richness and phenomenological openness have disappeared, and find instead meagre notes that give no picture of his world, but reduce him and his disease to a list of diagnostic criteria. (Silvers 1997)

In this book I will describe different syndromes, try to find the quality connected with each condition and search for the person behind the syndrome. If possible I hope that we can learn something from these syndromes.

I have shared my daily life now for more than 18 years with people who have many different kinds of developmental problems. In daily life, the diagnosis is not really relevant – what counts is the person – Mike, say, or Carla. As a doctor I often cannot help observing special characteristics, but these fade into the background when everyone celebrates Christmas together. Maybe this book seems too positive, sentimental even. Why not discuss the despair and pain of the parents, the insecurity for the future or the feelings of guilt? I didn't choose to write about the difficulties faced by the teacher, when it seems impossible to get a child to relax, when the child remains driven or imprisoned by his own obsessions and fears. Shouldn't I write about helping a youngster relate to his limitations? The youngster with developmental problems also has dreams about the future, but only a few of these youngsters will be able to marry, have children and live independent lives.

And then the real question: Where do parents and care-givers obtain the sustenance to go on with this difficult work? A large part of my work falls into these areas: to support parents, to help carers to understand the child better, to support the children in finding their own place in life. In this book I have tried to create a greater understanding for the person who lives with a genetic syndrome associated with a learning disability.

CHAPTER THREE

Genes and Behaviour

I have been living in Scotland now for several years. We have beautiful but rough hills here. On the hilltops the weather can be very
changeable, and it can often snow in spring and autumn. Many people are attracted to the challenge of these cold, windy, wintry places,
but it is still a shock to read in the newspapers every year of new trag-
edies – as in April 2000 when two climbers were found dead in the
Scottish hills. This brought that winter's total to fifteen deaths. Often
these are of healthy young people, mostly men.

Sometimes I like to look at the beautiful photographs of the shining *glitterati* in *Hello!* magazine. One issue, spring 2000, focused on a
young couple who were a bit unusual: she was the daughter of a duke,
brought up in luxury; he, a convicted bank robber. They had met in
prison: she was doing voluntary work, he was serving a sentence for
armed robbery. They talked in the magazine about the birth of their
second baby, which they were very much looking forward to, yet
weeks before the birth, he went off to climb – alone. He made it back
safely, but the trip was not without danger as five other climbers in the
same area never returned home during the same period.

Why am I telling this story? I was just reading Dean Hamer and
Peter Copeland's book, *Living with our Genes* (1998). This is a book
that discusses the crucial relationship between DNA and behaviour.
One of the behaviours looked at is novelty- or thrill-seeking behaviour. We are all different in terms of the level of excitement which
feels good to us: one person is happy sitting in front of the fireplace
with a book while another person goes abseiling. Research has now

shown that the degree of thrill-seeking behaviour is, to a certain extent, related to the length of a gene called the 'thrill-seeking gene'. I am sure the former bank robber and all those climbers have well-developed 'thrill-seeking genes' or 'novelty-seeking genes'. I would guess that the subject of this story used bank robbery as a thrill during the first part of his life, replacing it in the second half with a more socially acceptable form of thrill-seeking – climbing difficult hills.

It would be nice to think that such aspects of personality can be found in our genes. Luckily it is not so simple. There are many more genes involved with 'novelty-seeking', according to Harris (1995). Just 10 per cent of novelty-seeking would be related to this one specific gene. So how much do genes determine our behaviour? In the average person there are too many variations in the genetic make-up to discern clearly a determining gene. However, if you look at people with genetic syndromes and a learning disability, the story is different: we know more about their genetic make-up, but does that mean that we can also explain their behaviour by looking at their genetic differences?

It is clearly easier to research the link between genes and behaviour in people with special genetic syndromes, and so scientists are suddenly very interested in this group of people. My impression is that their interest is not simply to help these people in their development, rather they offer a unique opportunity for research into brain function, genetic disposition and behaviour. The fact is that there are aspects of a person with a genetic syndrome and learning disability that are influenced by their genetic condition. I would argue, however, that this doesn't do justice to the whole personality.

The history of genetic research

The history of research into the relationship between genes and behaviour is fascinating, but it also shows us the possible dangers. In 1866, Langdon Down, the doctor who first described Down Syndrome, also clearly described specific behaviours in his 'mongols'. At that point in history, this was not taken any further: the medical world at that time was not so interested in these observations. There was a special interest in a different discipline – eugenics. Francis Galton (1822–1911), a cousin of Charles Darwin, is the founder member of this movement.

'Eugenics' is the name given to the study of the inheritance of health and of how to stimulate 'favourable' human characteristics through 'breeding' whilst preventing the birth of people with 'unfavourable' characteristics. In America research flourished and families were described where 'negative' qualities were being passed on. One family is especially mentioned: the Kallikals. In this family were 143 people with learning disabilities, 26 illegitimate children, 33 prostitutes, 24 alcoholics and 3 criminals; 82 children died in infancy. Sterilization was practised on such families to 'protect the race'. Eugenics was also practised in Europe, but Britain never passed a 'eugenics law' – that is a law interfering with a person's right to breed. America was the first to pass such a law, followed by Sweden, Canada, Norway, Finland, Estonia and Iceland. Germany also practised eugenics, but Hitler took this a few steps further, with extreme consequences (Ridley 1999, pp.290–291).

After the Second World War the emphasis in genetic research moved away from genetic research and towards environmental influences. This was brought to an extreme when 'cold' mothers were perceived as the cause of conditions such as autism and schizophrenia (Nelkin and Lindee 1995; Jordan 1999).

In the 1970s interest in and knowledge of genetics increased. This had started with the first chromosomal disorder, Trisomy 21 or Down Syndrome, in 1957. In 1970 over 20 chromosomal disorders were known. The possibility of diagnosing small chromosmal disorders made further developments possible (Connor and Ferguson-Smith 1997). This development is reflected in the enormous increase in knowledge about genes. June 2000 saw the announcement that the mapping of the human genome by the 'Human Genome Project' had reached a 'first draft'. This is seen as a remarkable achievement, which will allow medical science to develop further, but there is also some concern as to what mankind will do with this knowledge. Who will want to know about genetic susceptibility for an illness if there is no cure?

Chromosomes

Human beings have 23 pairs of chromosomes, or 46 chromosomes in total. Of these, 22 pairs, chromosomes 1 to 22, are called 'autosomes'. The final pair are the sex chromosomes, which differ according to gender: males have both an X and a Y chromosome; females have an XX configuration. During meiosis (the formation of the sperm or ovum), the chromosomes split into two groups, leaving 23 chromosomes in the ovum or sperm. Each will provide half of the chromosomes for an embryo, should fertilization occur.

Genetics

Genes are part of an invisible, inherited genetic structure. They play an ever-increasing role, not only in the field of medical science but also in our culture. Insurance companies have already become very interested in our genetic structure. Soon, having a certain genetic predisposition may have huge financial consequences.

In Britain, it was recently agreed that insurance companies would be allowed to ask for the result of a genetic test for Huntingdon's Chorea, a dominant inherited disease that expresses itself in increasing problems with movement and dementia from the age of 30 to 40 and leads to an early death. The companies say that this will be to the advantage of people with this illness in the family as a negative test result will allow family members to obtain insurance, but how does that leave people with a positive test result?

Dorothy Nelkin and Susan Lindee describe the growing importance of genes in American culture in their book *The DNA Mystique* (1995). They analyse the image of genetics in popular culture, where DNA has been touted as an explanation for such things as personality, crime and individual success or failure. They show that genes have become a metaphor for everything in us. Genes have replaced the gods: our destiny is no longer to be read in the stars but in our genes.

Another important image of the gene in our culture is presented by Richard Dawkins, who wrote the book *The Selfish Gene* (1976). In this book, he calls human beings 'survival machines – robot vehicles that are blindly programmed to preserve the selfish molecules known as genes' (p.24). The authors of *The DNA Mystique* point out that although this appears very materialistic and anti-religious, it presents the image of DNA as immortal and the individual body as irrelevant. This resembles the religious approach of previous centuries, where belief was in the immortal soul and the unimportance of earthly matter.

The interpretation of medical genetic research is not always straightforward. Ruth Hubbard, a professor of biology, points to the dangers associated with faith in genetic predestination. She objects to efforts to explain living organisms in terms of 'important molecules' – namely, those in DNA (Hubbard and Wald 1997). This can lead to tendentious conclusions. She mentions research into males with the XYY chromosome variation (most males have an XY configuration). Around 1960, various articles were published about this group of men. The conclusion was that they were more often aggressive and criminal than other men: higher than expected percentages of prison inmates have this XYY configuration. Later, this turned out to be a false conclusion: men with XYY often lead a normal life, and the ones who are imprisoned often didn't commit any violent crime.

The science of genetics can have far-reaching consequences, which all the hubbub around the cloned sheep, Dolly (a cell from the udder of a sheep provided the genetic material for Dolly), made very clear. Suddenly the possibility of cloned human beings came into sight. What would be the consequences? Many people felt alarmed, and the then US President Bill Clinton asked for a moratorium on research into human cloning. On 20 December 2000, British newspaper headlines reported that members of parliament had voted to allow the cloning of human embryos up to 14 days old.

The central questions in all this remain: Do we live on in our genes? Do they contain the essence of our humanity? Scientists have determined that 98.4 per cent of human DNA is identical to the DNA of a chimpanzee. Would the remaining 1.6 per cent really contain all the information about our humanity, including our culture, music, language, literature and who knows what else? In fact, all humans share 99.9 per cent of the same genetic structure. So maybe there is more to us than our genes.

Genes

It is possible for us to visualize chromosomes, but how is that with genes? Who has ever seen a gene? The word 'gene' is frequently used, but the concept is not even a hundred years old. The biologist W. Johannsen introduced the 'gene' in 1909, but he did not make the connection to chromosomes – he just wanted to point out that inherited characteristics could be found in the sperm or egg cell.

In 1953 the physical substance of the gene was found: deoxyribonucleic acid (DNA). In the same year, James Watson and Francis Crick proposed a model for the structure of DNA. The 23 pairs of chromosomes are located in the nucleus of each of our cells, each chromosome consisting of strands of DNA forming a double helix. The backbone of this double helix is made up of repeating sugar and phosphate molecules. To each sugar molecule is attached one of four molecules or bases: Cytosine, Adenine, Guanine and Thymine, designated by the letters C, A, G and T. A group made up of a base, phosphate and a sugar is called a 'nucleotide'. Based on the principle that opposite complementary strands pair up, T is always paired with A, C always with G. The weak attraction or bonding between the two bases of the pair helps to hold the two strands of the helix together. It is this pairing and bonding of the bases combined with their linear distribution along the DNA strand, which makes it possible to determine the sequence of bases in DNA. The chromosomes vary in size, having 50–250 million base pairs each.

Watson (1968) wrote a lively book in which he described the atmosphere around the discovery of the double helix. He was just 25, an inquisitive young American. Crick is described as a sanguine, brilliant English scientist whose ideas had never yet led to anything great. After reading this book it became clear to me that this pioneering work would never have happened without the support of a wide group of scientists.

Many of us learnt this clear concept at school: DNA can produce a messenger, i.e. 'messenger RNA' or mRNA. This messenger produces a protein (enzyme) and this enzyme creates a specific characteristic.

DNA → mRNA → protein → characteristic

This 'central dogma of molecular biology' developed by Crick in 1950 seemed clear and straightforward, yet science moved on and the reality grew more complex. Nevertheless, the original theory was simple to understand, and since then newspaper articles have been based on its message. For instance, 'A new gene for obesity is discovered!'. The general public is not made aware that what we are being presented with is an oversimplification of reality.

The way genes work is much more complex than this simplified mechanism suggests. I attended a fascinating conference in Switzerland in 1997, called 'The Future of DNA'. This was a meeting place to discuss the different sociological and biological effects of the new developments in DNA. One of the speakers was a slightly built lady of Chinese origin, Mae-Wan Ho, who was a very powerful speaker. She pointed out that the mechanical and reductionist view of DNA has made it possible to gain knowledge and develop practical applications for recombining DNA. But, she stressed, this 'old paradigm of molecular biology' needs complementation. She put forward a point of view in which organisms are embedded in their environment, and DNA has a fluid quality to it. This means that DNA can be influenced by its environment, that the cause-and-effect between DNA and protein formation is not linear and direct but circular and non-linear (Wirz 1997).

We have been given the impression that genes have fixed identities, but this is far from the truth. Genes mean something different depending on the scientist, as David Heaf writes:

> A classical geneticist sees a gene as a unit of heredity transmitting different characteristics (e.g. eye colour) from parent to offspring according to Mendel's law of inheritance. To a molecular biologist it is a stretch of bases on a DNA strand that codes for a unit of function in the cell. An evolutionary biologist regards a

gene as a cell component robust enough to serve as the basis for evolution. And the biochemist's gene is a piece of DNA that the cell needs in order to make a protein. (Heaf 2000)

The gene concept gets even fuzzier when the following properties are considered: genes can split into several parts along the DNA chain or have base sequences which overlap with other genes. They often have no defined ends because of their associated flanking and control sequences. The fluidity of the genome and the so-called 'jumping genes' mean that genes often have no permanent location in chromosomes or DNA.

The overall conclusion of the conference in Switzerland was that the way we look at DNA can have far-reaching consequences. Focusing specifically on the consequences for people with a genetic syndrome, the danger is this: if we see DNA as all-determining and influential, it could prepare us for a new eugenic thinking, not organized from above by law, as in Hitler's Germany, but presented to us as a 'freedom of choice', which amounts to pressure from below – the pressure to conform. In this type of DNA thinking, people with genetic syndromes are mistakes of DNA, of recombination, and should be prevented from being born.

We never know the exact outcome of a certain genetic variation, so how can we give an opinion on the worth of such a person's life? What I will also illustrate in Chapters 13 and 14 is that the value of a life cannot only be measured by looking at a person's achievements: a person with a disability influences the environment, often not in a negative way. Another image to help us to understand genes could be this: genes could be likened to the letters of the alphabet. The old paradigm would see them as letters in a game of Scrabble – it does not matter where or when the game is played, the score depends on what the letters are worth. How different it is with the letters in a poem. The letters form words. Sometimes the words touch me, sometimes they leave me indifferent. Likewise, some genes touch a person deeply, as we will see in the next chapters.

People with genetically determined syndromes

The greatest struggle for me in writing this book has been trying to understand the enormous influence a specific genetic deletion (= missing a small part of a gene) or expansion (= one part of a gene has more repeats of a sequence of nucleotides) can have on a human biography, as is the case with Angelman Syndrome, Prader-Willi Syndrome and Fragile X Syndrome. It is easier to understand that an extra chromosome, as is the case in Down Syndrome, will have quite an influence on a person. My impression is that these specific genetic variations, found in some of these syndromes, limit the fluidity of the DNA and cause a loss in freedom for the person. I will explore this further in the next chapter: 'The First Smile'.

This is a book about people who are influenced by their genetic variation. Not only do they look different and have a degree of learning disability, but also their emotional reactions, social relationships and use of language are coloured by their condition. I have tried to describe the special characteristics of each syndrome on a physical level, a developmental level and an emotional level. Understanding all of this should enable us to find a better approach to the person. But most important of all, I work with the conviction that every person is unique, and their genetic constellation is a special way to express their uniqueness.

CHAPTER FOUR

The First Smile

Within Western culture, large families have become more or less a thing of the past. I grew up in a Roman Catholic region of Holland where large families are still quite common, but our family was small, with just 5 children. My husband has 10 siblings, nothing special in a street where the neighbours had 16 children. A few years ago, I met another large family: father, mother and 11 children. They were quite musical and had a family orchestra that would perform for us. I can't remember the music now, but I can still recall the children, aged 3 to 16, clearly. The younger children were all very similar – same haircut, same features – but when you looked at the 11 to 16-year-old children, things changed. They didn't look so similar any more, rather you saw that they were becoming individuals – youngsters with their own personality.

When we look at a newborn baby, it is usual to try to identify whether it resembles its mum or dad. We parents feel quite proud if the baby looks like us. I once received an unusual compliment for my third baby. A visitor looked at our baby son, then back at us and exclaimed, full of amazement: 'How did you get such a beautiful baby?'

Children are born into the hereditary stream of their parents and their race. Growing up means gradually developing more and more our own identity, until we usually leave our family and have to learn to stand on our own two feet and continue on our own path. That large family perfectly demonstrated to me the development of a person. But how does this process of individualization happen? How do we succeed in adapting this 'inherited body' and the environment where we grew up into our own individuality? Why do some people have more difficulty with this? Before we look at these issues, we first have to ponder the question: Where does a human being come from?

Life after death is nowadays quite a normal subject to discuss. For one person it is simply a reality, for another it is clear that we live on in our deeds, our children and our genes. It is not very often that people pay attention to the time before birth, or rather before conception. Is the human being created at conception or was he or she already present? In one-on-one conversations, some mothers discuss their own experiences with this, such as the busy mum of two with a full-time job who felt that her family was complete, except that she had a recurring dream about a child which she couldn't ignore. At last she gave in. She became pregnant, and when the child was born, it resembled the child in her dream.

This is just one story, but there are many more: Dietrich Bauer collected many similar anecdotes (Bauer 1986). If these stories are based on truth, then the theory of heredity takes on a different meaning. We could ask ourselves if the 'individual-to-be' chooses to be born into a specific family. Maybe she was born into this family because her 'soft knock' was not heard in another family. If we go deeper into this thought process, we can imagine that the hereditary stream that she was born into doesn't quite fit – the child needs to 'work through' her inherited body, make it her own. The older children in the family described above had been quite busy already with the process of individualization! Peter Grünewald describes this process, whereby a child slowly reveals its individuality, in a fascinating article (Grünewald 1997).

A newborn baby is incredibly open: it takes the world in intensely, and with a steady gaze. An important moment is when the first smile breaks through, when the child's face lights up for the first time and the serious expression has gone. At this time, the child truly enters our social environment. The Dutch poet Frederik van Eeden described this movingly in the poem, 'When our child smiled':

The very first time that our child smiled
He floated down from far, silent lands
Where he had not hearing, neither had he sight
And lived uniquely by an internal light.

I haven't yet found an English poem that describes so beautifully where a baby comes from. In the famous children's book *Mary Poppins in the Park* there is a chapter about the birth of Annabel, the fifth child in the family (Travers 1994). Annabel has just been born and is lying in her cradle. The crow comes to her and asks where she came from. Annabel replies: 'I am earth and air and fire and water; I come from the dark where all things have their beginnings'. The crow is very disappointed when, after a week, Annabel forgets about her origins.

In this first smile two processes can be seen: first, the response of the child to our smile; second, the mastery over its facial muscles. What freedom! What a radiant love! The infant, who up till now had a mostly peripheral consciousness, is slowly connecting to its own body. The chaotic movements which are determined by innate reflexes are being mastered. Gradually, the sensory impressions are less overwhelming and the child can relate more to those impressions and respond accordingly. Of course, this is all relative. Everybody who has seen a newly born infant is amazed by the clarity of the gaze with which it looks out into the world.

Professor Trevarthen, an eminent professor of child psychology and psychobiology, has done extensive research into early interaction with infants (Trevarthen *et al.* 1998). He shows that infants are born with an innate drive to communicate, that they have goals, interests and moral intentions. They are not a 'blank slate'. The child develops, learns to speak and name things in its surroundings. Next, the child starts to think and develop concepts. Through these processes the child slowly gains some independence and freedom. But if this process, separation from the world, were the only process, then we would be lonely. That is why it is also important to connect with the world. One way that children do this is through imitation: when we speak to a young baby, she moves her mouth; a toddler follows his mum through the house and wants to clean like mum. This imitation

is not only to the deeds and words of the adult, but also to the intentions behind them. Through this imitation a child achieves a connection to the world, and it is this imitation that is so painfully difficult
for a child with autism.

The process continues, and the child becomes more and more
self-directing. The child is in the process of growing up in a positive
manner. Every child responds differently to her impressions and her
environment, and the environment responds back to the child. Even
in a large family no two children have the same experience.

Why have I described all of this? Because growing up is never
straightforward. If you have developmental problems, then the process of 'taking hold' of your own body, of connecting to the surrounding world, is always altered. (I don't use the word disturbed –
disturbed would indicate that there is one right way to be, one right
way to develop; I believe that human beings exist in all colours and
expressions.) The differences are obvious in people with a genetic
syndrome and low intellectual ability – the motor development does
not happen freely, the personality cannot express itself totally, certain
gestures become characteristic for the syndrome, the ability to transform sensory impressions into concepts, thoughts, etc. is limited. In
certain syndromes, for example in Down Syndrome, there is often too
much invitation and openness to the environment. Think of the typical, very friendly, open attitude of a person with Down Syndrome.
The hypersensitivity of a person with Fragile X Syndrome also demonstrates a very strong connection with the surroundings. In other
syndromes, Prader-Willi Syndrome for example, there is a difficulty,
or even inability, to see things from somebody else's point of view.

Human beings are so fascinating because we develop, have new
experiences and can learn new skills. I find nothing more moving
than to witness a child making a new step in his development. We all
remember the joy when a baby learns to walk. In children a promise
of future development is made visible. How do we, as grown-ups,
manage to keep this promise, the possibility for growth, alive? It
seems almost as if, when development is broken, the uniqueness of
the person becomes hidden and a certain greyness descends.

Let us summarize all of this: self-development is the process by which the individuality slowly penetrates the emotional life, habits, life processes and finally the physical body, maybe even the genetic structure (Grünewald 1997). The degree to which we manage to form our own biography indicates how far we manage to do this. If this process is just partially successful then a different process happens: the physical, inherited body starts to determine our habits, our feelings, our life and behaviour. Our individuality is then difficult to notice. We can experience this to a certain extent in people who continue to resemble their father or mother strongly into adulthood. For people with a genetic syndrome this plays quite a strong role. The extra chromosome or lack of certain genes influences how they look, move and respond with their feelings. It often takes extra effort to meet the individual who lives with one of these syndromes.

Every person is unique, and has their own biography; this is of course true of people with a genetic syndrome too. If you are aware of the specific 'colour' a syndrome gives to a person, then you can accept the person better and can be more helpful. It is even possible that a person with a syndrome needs help so that his individuality has a stronger grip on his feelings, behaviour, habits and body. The image provided by Truida de Raaf illustrates this well: she compares the human being to a horse-drawn carriage (Niemeyer et al. 1999). The carriage is the image of a body: it can be damaged, beautiful or ugly. The horses symbolize the soul: they can be well trained and fiery or neglected and difficult to control. The driver, holding the reins, symbolizes individuality: he or she has to work with the given carriage and horses.

Figure 4.1 demonstrates de Raaf's point clearly. In every person there is an interplay between what we glean from life – our experiences and environment – and our personality. (The environmental influences, such as family, country of residence, nutrition, are left out of Figure 4.1 for simplicity.) In people with a genetic syndrome, genetics can play a stronger role than the other elements.

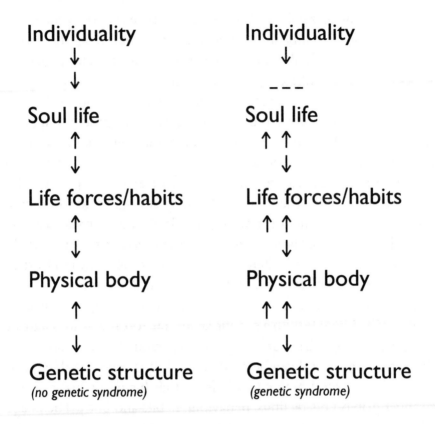

Figure 4.1 The impact of a genetic syndrome on personality

Good behaviour/bad behaviour

The new student's psychiatrist was discussing her 'good' and 'bad' behaviour. Is this a good approach to take? It implies a freedom: the possibility to choose how one behaves. But behaviour can be a symptom of underlying fear, insecurity, tension, pain, rage or disappointment. It is always interesting to see how the presence of certain people who know a child and can create a feeling of security can make a difference, especially for children with unexpected and difficult behaviour, and strong mood swings.

Take Kevin, quite a difficult youngster, who could hit and kick young carers and bring them to the point of despair. Yet if you met him in the company of an experienced, older carer, you would see a different person – one who could be pleasant and co-operative, although he clearly still had his learning disability. He had learned to control his own emotional life through the presence of an experienced carer. It is logical that this is not so easy when he was with a young carer, whose own personality might not yet be fully developed. The hope was that Kevin would learn to find some peace in himself so that he was not so dependent on the presence of an experienced carer. This indeed happened over the years, and he matured and calmed down quite considerably.

In the process of growing up and developing self-knowledge, the most important element is the support of a trusting adult. Usually this is the parent, but a teacher, carer or befriender may also be important. Education which includes an artistic component, a structured daily life, and sometimes religion, can be helpful in giving support. If a child with developmental problems needs more support, then specific therapies can be offered: art therapy, rhythmical massage, music therapy, counselling, play therapy, movement therapy (eurythmy) and horse-riding.

Life is never easy for anyone, let alone for those who arrive in this world being 'different'. It starts with the disappointment, shock and anger that parents experience when they realize that their child has a genetic syndrome. These feelings gradually find their place and the parents form a deep attachment with their child, but the infant will sense these confused feelings. Later the child will be aware of strange looks or teasing. Although children with a genetic syndrome and intellectual disability are not always so very intelligent, they are quite sensitive to the atmosphere around them. They sense the pain that their difficulties can cause. Sometimes their own pain is hidden behind a smile, as in the case of David, in Chapter 9 on Foetal Alcohol Syndrome. The reactions from their environment and failures in school can mean an extra challenge in life. Marie, a woman with Down Syndrome, touched me deeply when she described how unhappy she was in her youth.

In the following chapters I have included some biographical descriptions. I will try to show how the children described have struggled to achieve self-determination and how they were supported in this.

CHAPTER FIVE

Down Syndrome
What's in a Name?

Jo Harris is a young woman with Down Syndrome who made headlines in Britain in the autumn of 2000. Millions of people watched with bated breath to see who would be the winner of the television series *Big Brother*. More than 3.5 million people voted Craig Philips the winner of the £70,000 prize. And when Craig announced that he was giving his prize money to Jo to help her obtain a heart and lung transplant, they all knew that they had made a good choice. Through his act Craig Phillips brought Down Syndrome to the attention of millions of people in Great Britain.

It was a bit of a gloomy, grey day one summer. We took the car and went to the local village in Brittany. While we waited at the traffic lights, a young man passed by the car. His head was slightly bent, his gait appeared a little heavy, he had beautiful small ears and an open, friendly disposition. He appeared so familiar to me, so well known, that I couldn't help greeting him. His response chased the greyness of the day away. He stopped, looked at me and greeted me full of enthusiasm.

We find it easy to recognize people with Down Syndrome. There are an enormous number of them – 1 in every 600–700 live births has this syndrome.

History

No book written before the nineteenth century contains a description of anyone with Down Syndrome. Did it not exist? Or did the children not survive because of poor hygiene and lack of medical care? We know these children are quite vulnerable to infectious diseases. At the beginning of the twentieth century the average survival rate for a person with Down Syndrome was only 9 years. Now the average age is 45 years.

Brian Stratford, however, describes how around the Gulf of Mexico drawings were found of short-built people who clearly had features of this condition (Stratford 1989). These drawings go back 1000 years before Christ. The people depicted were adored as supernatural beings – men and women who retained a child-like quality. Stratford also mentions a painting of a child with Down Syndrome as the Jesus child in the painting 'Madonna and Child' by the fifteenth century painter Mantegna.

We have of course to remember that there was limited interest in people with developmental problems until the nineteenth century. The only classification that was known was 'dementia' or 'idiocy' (congenital developmental problems). One of the first to become interested in the study of people with developmental disabilities was a man named Langdon Down (1828–1896). He grew up in Cornwall, went to school until the age of 13 and then started work in his father's apothecary. At the age of 25, after the death of his father, he studied medicine. His first place of work was in a large institution for 'idiots'. While working there, he noticed a similarity between many of his patients. The resemblance of these patients to one another was infinitely greater than to the members of their own families. He described it as follows:

> The face is flat and broad and destitute of prominence. The eyes are obliquely placed. These children always have great power of imitation and become extremely good mimics. They have a feeling for humour. They can learn much more than expected. (Down 1990, pp.5–8)

Many of Down's observations still hold true today. His most important contribution was in helping people with learning disabilities achieve their potential through education and training.

Down thought that many people with Down Syndrome showed similarities to people from the Mongolian race, so he called them 'mongols'. He did this also to move away from the classification 'idiot' which was the main one used until then. He first described Down Syndrome in the second half of the nineteenth century, and the recognition of Down Syndrome spread – first through England and Scotland, later through Central Europe and over the whole world.

Chromosomes

The middle of the twentieth century saw a renewed interest in developmental problems. It had been assumed until that time that every human being had 48 chromosomes. In 1956 J.H. Tjio and A. Levan discovered that normally people have 46 chromosomes in every cell (Connor and Ferguson-Smith 1997). Because of this discovery, Lejeune and colleagues were able to diagnose Trisomy 21 as the first chromosome abnormality: they found that people with Down Syndrome have 47 chromosomes. Other chromosomal abnormalities were later described (Connor and Ferguson-Smith 1997).

With this discovery the discussion regarding the appropriate name for 'Down Syndrome' was rekindled – should it be Mongolism, Down Syndrome or Trisomy 21? The name Down Syndrome was adopted, and will probably stay the official name.

Genetic background

Down Syndrome can be caused by three different genetic situations:

- The most common, i.e. in 95 per cent of cases, is 'non-dysfunction'. During the formation of an egg or sperm, two Chromosomes 21 are formed in the nucleus. If fertilization occurs, the foetus receives a total of 47 chromosomes, including three Chromosomes 21 instead of two. This cannot be inherited. It is still not known why non-dysfunction happens and why it is more often the egg cell which has two Chromosomes 21. It is general knowledge that the possibility of having a Down Syndrome child increases as the mother gets older.

- 'Translocation' happens in 1–5 per cent of the cases. In this case the person with Down Syndrome has 46 chromosomes, but to one of the chromosomes, often Chromosome 14, is attached a large part of Chromosome 21, with the result that the person has the genetic information of Chromosome 21 three times. This translocation mostly happens spontaneously, although sometimes it has been passed on from the mother, in which case the mother has a 25 per cent chance of having a second child with Down Syndrome.

- The third form is 'Mosaicism'. This chromosome variation happens in just 1 or 2 per cent of cases. Some cells of the person with Down Syndrome will have 46 chromosomes, others 47 chromosomes. I was acquainted with a man with this condition. He did not have the typical features of Down, had mild learning difficulties and was outgoing and sociable.

Theory

How is it possible that an extra Chromosome 21 leads to the typical characteristics seen in Down Syndrome? There is quite a range of expression in this syndrome, but the features are easily recognizable. Richard Phethean, a pharmacist and parent of a girl with Down Syndrome who lives in one of the Camphill communities, summarizes it as follows in an article in the *Curative Journal*. I include part of the article, with his consent.

Conventional understanding of Down Syndrome has led us to believe that it is a genetic disorder that is a *fait accompli*, and that therefore there is little more that can be done to help the situation. There can easily arise an attitude of just accepting that they are who they are, and not much more can be or needs to be done.

In Down Syndrome there is an extra 21st chromosome leading to a genetic overload. As genes create enzymes and proteins, this extra chromosome, which then occurs in each cell in the body, causes a number of metabolic imbalances due to too many enzymes and proteins. These lead to the typical Down characteristics: the underdeveloped nose, the Asiatic facial appearance, small growth, waddled gait, difficulty in running, sparse straight hair, underdeveloped jaws, flattened upper lip, often short-sightedness or crossed eyes, and the floppy, ragdoll feel. One can liken Down Syndrome to a cake recipe with too many ingredients. The 'short' ingredients can be added to balance out the 'extra' ingredients. In other words, nutrition can be used to compensate for the genetic overdose.

Researchers have begun to recognise that Down children share similar metabolic disturbances. The heart of the problem is abnormal levels of antioxidant enzymes – too little catalase and too much superoxide dismutase (SOD). This causes a profound disturbance of the antioxidant defence system. Ordinarily, levels of SOD, whose job is to mop up free radicals and convert them to hydrogen peroxide, exist in subtle harmony with catalase and glutathione peroxidase. But where there is too much SOD produced, the body overproduces hydrogen peroxide, which builds up in the cells, and breaks down further into more free radicals. When there aren't enough antioxidant enzymes to detoxify this H_2O_2, the dietary antioxidants we take in as food must finish the job. The most important dietary antioxidants are vitamins A, C and E, beta-carotene, co-enzyme Q and the minerals zinc and selenium. (Beta-carotene is provitamin A and is an important antioxidant.) Many children and adults with Down Syndrome exhibit profound deficiencies of the antioxidant nutrients vitamin A, E, C, zinc, selenium and glutathione. Further, research has shown that when these substances are given to people with Down Syndrome, they disappear from the blood much more rapidly than usual. With low levels of antioxidants, free radical production runs riot in each cell, causing problems with many major bodily functions.

Oxidative free radicals are chemical entities that are often found in the cell environment; being highly reactive, they can cause serious damage within the cell. They are found in larger amounts as a result of pollution, smoke, e.g. from barbecues or cigarettes, radiation, ozone, and even stress. In a normal person, these are fairly effectively inactivated by a series of enzymes and anti-oxidant vitamins. It seems that this mechanism in the Down Syndrome metabolism is deficient, and the excess of free radicals causes damage to enzymes, DNA and the cell wall. The damage to the cell wall is of particular consequence for the brain and nervous system, where it causes loss of the transmission of nerve impulses and a more rapid than normal loss of neurones in the brain. Obviously this can result in a wide variety of effects from poor motor coordination, low IQ to memory loss and the early onset of senile dementia (Alzheimer's disease) which is often seen in Down Syndrome. The cell wall is predominantly lipid (fatty) substance. The brain is also predominantly composed of lipid substance, the most common of which is docosahexaenoic acid (DHA), a highly unsaturated fatty acid. By including in the diet the correct essential fatty acids, such as Omega 3 unsaturated oil as found in flax seed (linseed) oil as well as DHA, found in fish oils, the damage to the cell walls caused by the free radicals can be more rapidly repaired. This is vital if progressive brain degeneration is to be avoided. The typical physical appearance of the brain of a 40-year-old person with Down Syndrome has the same characteristics as that of a person with Alzheimer's disease, even if dementia is not present. Trials have shown that vitamin E, one of the most powerful antioxidants known, is effective in delaying the onset of Alzheimer's disease and maintaining memory function in old age.

Immune system

People with Down Syndrome supposedly have a 52 times greater incidence of infections compared with normal people, which is largely due to the poorly functioning immune system caused by oxidative stress (excess of *oxidative* free radicals) and low levels of antioxidants. With a normal diet, the typically low to normal levels of antioxidant vitamins are being rapidly used up, which leads to low blood levels. The Down Syndrome person simply needs a higher intake of these nutrients in order to maintain adequate blood levels and a healthy immune system. Independent research on normal people has shown that vitamins A, C and E, zinc and selenium all help to improve resistance to infection.

Other researchers have found lower levels of B vitamins in Down Syndrome. One of the main functions of the B group of vitamins is to maintain the healthy function of the nervous system.

Nutritional Therapy

The pioneer of the nutritional approach is Dr Henry Turkel, who developed Targeted Nutritional Intervention (TNI) more than 50 years ago. Dr Turkel developed a programme he called his 'U series' – a compilation of vitamins, minerals, digestive enzymes, essential fatty acids, amino acids and several drugs, including thyroid hormone. He managed to get approval to sell his programme in Michigan and treated some 5000 patients, reportedly with some success.

The current recommendation for therapy consists of administering a supplement containing a broad spectrum of vitamins, minerals, amino acids and digestive enzymes, at doses close to or slightly higher than recommended daily allowances, but well within recognized safe limits.

Diet

Research has shown that most children with Down's Syndrome are lactose intolerant, and do better on a milk-free diet (although some dairy products like cheese and yoghurt may be OK). Milk also contains vitamin D2, which is not well tolerated. Dr König advocated a dairy-free diet for them. It is known that milk products increase the production of mucus, which increases the Down Syndrome person's tendency to bronchial infections. Doctors in Germany have reported that post-mortem examinations performed on people with Down Syndrome brought to light many cases of advanced bronchial infections which had not been previously diagnosed. Also, many are gluten intolerant, i.e. have coeliac disease. This results in damage to the lining of the small intestine, poor absorption of vital nutrients and severe digestion disorders. If this is the case, then complete avoidance of wheat, rye, barley and oats is the only known treatment. Further, a diet high in animal fats can result in reduced levels of the essential fatty acid DHA, which is vital for a healthy nervous system.

People with Down Syndrome often have a weaker digestion than normal which can result in malabsorption of foodstuffs including vitamins etc. It is likely that larger than normal quantities of essential nutrients need to be given. TNI includes digestive enzymes, which help with the correct digestion of carbohydrates, proteins and fats. It also includes specific amino acids (the building blocks of proteins) in order to compensate for digestive weakness and to supply those, which are most lacking as a result of their faulty metabolism.

Observed effects of Targeted Nutritional Intervention

There are far fewer infections, resulting in fewer days off school. The immune system is enhanced, as shown by blood levels of white blood cells and immunoglobulines. There is often an improvement in speech, gross motor and fine motor coordination and cognition. Intelligence (IQ) has been shown to be enhanced by some researchers, but many are wary of making claims in this direction partly so as not to build up the hopes of parents. Most parents report more normal growth, better muscle tone, thickening of hair, more supple skin and changes of the facial features to a more normal appearance. In some cases, photographs of children with Down Syndrome cannot be recognized as having the syndrome at all.

Recently a review article was published (Ani, Grantham-McGregor and Muller 2000) which showed that neural cells of aborted foetuses with Down Syndrome showed a fourfold increase of free radicals and a twofold increase of SOD (superoxidase dismutase). It was also found that a increase of SOD is related to higher level of apoptosis, or cell death. So it is very likely that the nerve cells of a baby with Down Syndrome are limited in their growth development before birth.

But there is no good scientific research yet which can show that nutritional supplementation works. The conclusion of the article is that a double blind trial with 170 individuals with Down Syndrome is required, half whom are treated and the other half not. The Down Syndrome Research Association is trying to set this up but still lacks funding at the time of writing. Ironically, I find, money for prenatal diagnosis is easily available, but not for research into treatment.

All this makes me wonder whether there are metabolic disturbances in the other syndromes and if one day a targeted treatment will be available for them.

Karl König

Karl König, a doctor and founder of the Camphill movement, had a special connection to people with Down Syndrome. Fifty years ago, König tried to understand the destiny of these people. It was clear that he saw people with this condition not as disabled, but as different. He developed the idea that these people have retained general human characteristics – they have not totally individualized their destiny. They are less desirous of prestige, money or an exalted position in life but live more in the 'now'.

A mother who brought her child with Down Syndrome to the Camphill schools 40 years ago described how children with Down Syndrome were revered. It was seen as an honour to have a child with Down Syndrome in a class or house community because of the warmth and humanity they radiated. Is this still the case now?

For one thing, people with Down Syndrome are more individualized, more 'down to earth' and have more opportunities to develop than ever. Kerri illustrates this clearly. She is an active, outgoing young woman of 23 years who has a keen interest in life. Her interests extend to young men, and she is surely hoping to have a relationship, even a physical relationship. She gives the impression of being really connected to reality. It was therefore quite a revelation for me when the art therapist showed me Kerri's work. Karl König gave the image of Down Syndrome people as 'people from paradise'. This was clearly revealed in Kerri's artwork. Kerri drew herself as a heavenly being in the air, without legs. In a second drawing she depicted herself as a flower. It made me wonder how people with Down Syndrome really experience themselves.

I interviewed Kerri to ask about her life. She told me: 'I have some problems.' She then described some difficulties in her work place-ment. I told her I was writing about Down Syndrome, and if she knew what that was. 'I have never heard about it', she replied. Then she continued:

> I get quite jealous easily. I have been here [a residential training place for young adults] for six years. I am coming to the end of my stay. I came at 17, I am 23 now. I quite enjoy it. I want to change my room. I am quite independent. I have a boyfriend now. I get on very well. Another girl is jealous about it. I am on a waiting list to go to Newton Dee [a village community for adults with special needs]. It will happen soon. I like to sort myself out, not to argue the whole time. He [the boyfriend] can't see me the whole time. I like to write e-mails, we have got a telephone with a computer screen. I have been in the Garden [as a work placement] for six years. I like it, especially in the spring. I like to talk to people, be friendly. I find it difficult to leave friends, makes me sad, uncomfortable.

> I am very independent now. I could look for a flat with my boy-friend and go for work in a day centre.

I asked: 'Did you discuss this with him?'

> No, I didn't. I am very independent with my money. I have to learn to cross the road. I am good at acting and playing. My mum is very nice to my boyfriend, she takes him out to watch

the salmon jump and eat chips. Sometimes I visit his parents' house.

Kerri describes the hopes and problems of any young woman. There is still a certain lack of self-awareness and it is easy to overestimate her intellectual abilities. She has often heard her mother talking about Down Syndrome, but it hasn't sunk in: it is not a reality for her. She doesn't experience herself as different. The fact that she lives in a residential community where there are quite a number of others with Down Syndrome surely contributes to that. Her boyfriend and her best friends have this same condition.

Kerri and I looked through all her photos to see which one would be suitable for inclusion in this book. 'I would like to be famous,' she told me. And why not? The photo shows Kerri at her best, full of confidence, energy and enthusiasm.

A Camphill art therapist and I explored this further and talked to more people with this constitution, and in their drawings we could see the theme of not being connected to earth, hovering above the earth, recurring.

So it is very appropriate that the people with Down Syndrome have a column about themselves in the Down's Association magazine, which they call 'Down to Earth!' They want to be down to earth, and our task is to help facilitate this, while still valuing the special qualities they bring along.

Down Syndrome: prenatal testing and destiny

One amazing aspect of this condition is the relentless effort the medical world is putting into preventing people being born with Down Syndrome. Of course, you are free as a parent to choose or not to choose prenatal diagnosis, but the general expectation is to go down this road. The risk for a child with Down Syndrome is greater the older the mother. The risk is 1 in 2300 when the mother is aged 20 rising to 1 in 100 when she is aged 40. There are different tests available to screen for Down Syndrome. It is possible to do a blood test on the mother to test for certain substances in her blood (a fetoprotein,

Kerri on holiday, aged 23

unconjugated oestriol, human chorionic gonadotrophin, and inhibin A) and to do an ultrasound and measure the thickness of the skinfold in the neck of the foetus (this is called nuchal translucency ultrasound measurement: the skin of the neck is thicker in a foetus with Down Syndrome). These results are combined with the risk associated with the age of the mother. If it is calculated from this that there is a definite risk of Down Syndrome, then amniocentesis (sampling of the cells of the unborn baby for genetic testing) will happen. Different clinics use different methods and it is not yet clear which is the most effective.

A future method will be to look for foetal cells in the mother's blood, which would be 100 per cent conclusive. Technically this is already possible but not yet on a large scale. So, will this mean that very soon no children with Down Syndrome will be born?

It is interesting for me to read the magazine of the Down Syndrome Association. Most parents describe the same process: how at first they are, of course, shocked but later deeply touched by their child with Down Syndrome. Their experience is that the children bring joy and love. In April 1997 I read in *Libelle*, a Dutch women's magazine, a letter from a grandmother to her grandchild which encompasses it all:

Life is a gift

My son phoned to tell me that you are a child with Down Syndrome. My first impressions were right after all. I was left with mixed feelings: happiness (my first grandchild) but also insecurity for 'the future'. These feelings didn't last long. You have developed into a healthy two-year-old child. You are lovely and affectionate, you laugh a lot, dance to music. I realise more and more that you have come to us to teach us, to show us that life is more than possession, hard work, prestige and stress.

Your proud Granny

The person with the condition

Langdon Down described not only the physical characteristics of people with Down Syndrome but also their behaviour. He was a keen observer, and some of his remarks still hold true. There is a danger, though, of stereotyping these people – not every person with this condition is extrovert and has a happy disposition. Karl König remarked that there are as many people with Down Syndrome who have an extrovert character as an introvert character, and many have a mixed soul disposition. The people who are more 'inward' often maintain the warmth to their behaviour, they never become distant.

Physical characteristics

The facial features are easily recognizable. The flattened middle face, small nose and ears, the slanted eyes, the small head which is flatter at the back, the tongue which can be quite large and the skin which is dry and easily reddened and irritated. The children are relatively small with short arms. The muscles are quite lax and the joints can be over-stretched. The thyroid often functions insufficiently and treatment is necessary. In 50 per cent of the cases cardiac problems can be present.

Development

A child with this constitution develops like any other baby, just at a slower rate. It can be difficult for the newborn baby to stay warm enough. The child will be weak and hypo-tonic and can have difficulties with drinking, but most mothers say that they are lovely babies.

I am normally involved with school children, so it was quite special to attend a busy study day on Down Syndrome in London. Many parents took their young babies along. Their floppiness and especially their quietness struck me; other babies of that same age would have been more lively and noisy. It seemed as if they did not have the energy to make many sounds.

Because of their slow development, the difference with other children becomes more and more apparent. The girls seem quicker than the boys. Also the motor development happens at a slower pace; sitting and walking will happen later than with other children.

Speech development

This is a specific problem. Most children are capable and alert in social settings but the speech can be difficult to understand or not developed enough. The consonants are often not pronounced clearly and there is an emphasis on the vowels (A, E, I, O, U). This use of language illustrates the general inner attitude of meeting life openly, full of sympathy. Compare it with the opposite situation – the very formed use of language of the English nobility with the emphasis on consonants, which creates a more distant impression.

Some of these children really have aphasia: they cannot form words. I remember a girl who was socially interactive when observed from a distance. Only later did it become clear to me that she could not speak but compensated with a lively use of signs.

The fact that many of these children have 'glue ear' (fluid behind their eardrums) does not help the speech development. This is the case in 80 per cent of these children. The reduced hearing, coupled with the increased time required for mental processing, is part of the reason for this slow speech development. However, it is not just the speech that is slow. If a mother tries to interact with her young baby and wants to make him smile, then the mother needs to be prepared to wait longer for a response. Buckley (quoted in O'Brien and Yule 1995) discovered that many of these children have an increased capacity to learn to read in their pre-school years. This can help their speech development.

Relationship between head and limbs

It may help us to understand people with Down Syndrome if we observe the bodily proportions of a child with Down Syndrome more closely. The head is on the small side with a flat occiput. The facial features are not always very individualized. The visual and auditory senses can be limited by hearing problems and reduced visual activity, and the intellect is clearly restricted, all of which somehow points to the fact that the 'head pole' is not the dominant part of the body. The limbs are smaller than average. Hands and feet are not so well formed. The poor muscle tone is well documented. The emphasis of the bodily build is in the thorax – the physical problems tend to be in this area. There is a tendency to become overweight and congenital heart abnormalities are a frequent feature. Bronchitis is also not uncommon.

An image arises of people who are not specifically skilled intellectually or in practical ways. It also appears that the quality of heart and lungs are not strong in the bodily realm but have freed themselves for the social life. This is the realm where people with this condition make their special, often not so visible but still important, contributions.

Behavioural problems

I should not paint too rosy a picture. There can be some behavioural problems. Research by Green and others in 1989 (cited in Harris 1995) showed that 25 per cent of young children have behavioural problems.

Donald is an example of a child with Down Syndrome. He is 9, small and round with a friendly open smile. The moment he doesn't want something, he flops down to the ground and will not move. He cannot speak but can produce quite a howling sound. If you are not aware of him for a split second he will manage to pull somebody's hair or smash a glass – for him this is great fun! If you leave him with a piece of string, he will dangle with it for hours and hypnotize himself. He has autism as well as Down Syndrome.

Jonas is another young man with this condition. He was quite a difficult teenager at 13 when he arrived at Camphill. He was the youngest of a large family with an older, protective mother. He could not speak, was not toilet-trained and could be wild and uncontrolled. The first day some plant pots were broken. After two years, however, we saw quite a change. He is mostly toilet-trained and can go to the workshop without a personal carer. In his workshop he is part of a team of youngsters who work together, outside on a project – a remarkable change. Was it the horse-riding therapy that did the trick, or the fact that he was addressed in an age-appropriate manner? Or did the complementary medicines help? Maybe all of these played a role, but the most important element was the dedicated but structured care of a good carer.

There is another, quite typical behaviour in these children: suddenly they can sit down on their bottom in the Buddha posture, whether in the room, the passage or during a walk, and nothing will get them going again. This would happen with Connie, a sturdy 14-year-old. The only solution was to take a small cart along, so that she could be put in there if she refused to walk.

The introvert Daniel could sit for hours on the floor of the toilet. When encouraged to get up he might answer with a polite 'No thank you', but at other times in a different mood he could escape and run off.

In general, I find people with this constitution to be good company and that is an experience that is shared by many in our school community. People with Down Syndrome have a directness in relating to other people, a certain warmth, that doesn't imply that they always want to be sociable in company.

Adult life and ageing

Nowadays people with Down Syndrome live longer than ever. When they reach the age of 20 a new vulnerability can come to the fore. Some young adults will become depressed and confused – it can even happen that they never recover from this. Some doctors have noticed that it seems to happen more often to the more capable youngsters. The reason is not clear. Is too much being expected? Is this a time of self-reflection, of awareness of destiny?

The gene for Alzheimer's disease is located on Chromosome 21. The brain of every person with Down Syndrome shows signs of this after the age of 35, but it will not be outwardly visible in every case. 40 per cent of those over 45 will show signs of some difficult behaviour: they become chaotic, difficult to entertain and have major concentration problems.

My hope (and that of others) is that Targeted Nutritional Intervention will help people with Down Syndrome to live even longer without dementia. Just remember that the average age of death 100 years ago was 9 years, not 45! Personally I know quite a number of independent healthy adults with this constitution who are 40 or 50, and they are all good company.

Openness as a way of self-realization

I discussed in Chapter 4 two streams of development in a child's life. One is getting into your bodily nature – connecting with your body; the other stream is connecting with the outside world. In Down

Syndrome it seems that the separation from the world is especially difficult. Also, intellectual development appears delayed; but more and more articles are appearing which show how people with Down Syndrome have made exceptional achievements, often thanks to an intensive training programme. Intense stimulation in the mental and physical realm prove helpful, such as for a woman with Down Syndrome in Holland who passed her standard grades (equivalent to British GCSEs) in 1997. These intensive programmes encourage the individual to get into their body.

The connection to the world around is quite well developed in most people with this constitution. Recently, I observed a young well-dressed Down teenager rollerblading. When a young child fell nearby and started crying, none of the other teenagers responded, except the young man with Down who comforted the child.

I want to conclude this chapter by letting a person with Down Syndrome include his opinions. Patrick Smith wrote in the *Observer* on 18 June 1994 in a letter:

> I don't believe they should abort children with Down's Syndrome. I don't believe the life of a baby should be taken because of Down's Syndrome. I am a human being like everybody else and should be treated as such. I am happy at the moment. I have reasons to be proud. I have been in the same job in the same factory for 30 years. I relate easily to people. I realised this when I went to the Café Royal last week to receive a Recognition. It was beautiful, like being in heaven only without the halo.

CHAPTER SIX

Williams Syndrome

Oliver Sacks, the well-known neurologist, made a programme about Williams Syndrome in the television series *Mind Traveller*. While watching I became increasingly intrigued. A young girl called Heidi was filmed and she seemed familiar to me; her openness, her direct-ness in contact, the open gaze mingled with some anxiety, the fluent use of language, even her intonation was familiar, as well as her way of behaving. After the programme finished I went directly to my old clinical notes; indeed, the girl whom Heidi reminded me of also had Williams Syndrome. Scientists are very interested in this rare syn-drome. It occurs in just 1 in 20,000–25,000 live births, with the same number of boys as girls being affected.

History

Williams Syndrome is named after the cardiologist R. Williams. He identified four children with aortic stenosis, learning disability and unusual facial appearance (Williams *et al.* 1961), but the syndrome was recognized earlier. After the Second World War quite a number of children in Europe suffered from hypercalcaemia. This seemed to be caused by too high a dosage of vitamin D in the infants' food. Most children were just mildly affected but there was a small group of children who suffered more from the hypercalcaemia. These children had an 'elf-like' face, learning disability and a congenital heart abnor-mality. These were the children with Williams Syndrome. It is an open question for me whether Langdon Down, the doctor who described children with Down Syndrome, points to Williams Syndrome. In one of his lectures he mentions: 'I have had under my care children with characteristic malar bones, prominent eyes, puffy lips and retreating skins. They have had woolly hair.'

Before writing this chapter, I was not aware of an article published in 1964 by two of my medical predecessors, George von Arnim and Peter Engel, which was about this syndrome and independent of other research. At that time, six children with Williams Syndrome were residential boarders in a school which gave a unique opportunity for close observation. The two doctors described the unusual linguistic ability and sociable, outgoing nature of these children, coupled with a background of fear and anxiety. They compared these children to children with Down Syndrome, who present a different picture regarding their emotional responses: Down children are often not verbally gifted but give the impression of feeling settled and safe (von Arnim and Engel 1964).

Physical characteristics

You can instantly recognize people with Williams Syndrome, once you are familiar with it. The face has a broad forehead, depressed nasal bridge with an upturned nose, widely spaced teeth and full lips. The prominent cheeks add to the typical Williams Syndrome face. The birth weight is low and growth retardation as a baby is a problem. The children can have digestive problems, are very sensitive to sound and can have congenital heart abnormalities. There is generally a developmental delay.

Personality

As I mentioned before, scientists are especially interested in Williams Syndrome because of its unique combination of characteristics. These are children and adults who speak fluently (although you would notice a difference with typically developing children), are superficially open, appear socially inclined and with an ear for music (this means they like music, but they are not as musical as children without developmental problems). On the other hand, they have a degree of learning disability and poor spatial orientation. Their drawings are only poorly formed compared with other people with a similar degree of disability. They have difficulties with concentration. Life is not always easy for children with this syndrome; they can have emotional and behavioural problems. It is difficult for them to make friends despite their social abilities and as children they relate better to adults. The diagnosis is often already made in infancy via genetic tests. Typically, the baby is a poor eater, irritable and constipated. A small percentage of them has too high a calcium level in the blood. This calcium level can be normalized with diet but this does not really change the behavioural and physical characteristics.

Alistair

The person I knew best with Williams Syndrome was Alistair. When I got to know him he was 40 and in a wheelchair. He lived with his mother in a local Camphill village community for adults. He had survived a brain haemorrhage at the age of 33 but couldn't walk any more and was frail. So his favourite activity was watching all the customers going to the Camphill village shop and talking to them. On good days he sat outside in the lovely flower garden and he sat by the window when the weather was bad. His mother wrote the following description of him when he was 48:

> Alistair has a short concentration span. His hearing is very acute, he can distinguish every musical instrument in an orchestra. He still covers his ears to blot out certain sounds.
>
> He has no particular friend – he likes his own company although he is outwardly friendly to all. He seems to read people. He can be approached with humour. He can't be asked a direct question but in his own time can recall and tell a great deal. He has a somewhat reserved nature and is not demonstrative. He is not very interested in things – people and living in company, even as an onlooker, is his forte. He has been on his special diet and never has complained and always thanks people for what he has had.

He has little concept of up and down, right and left or back and front. His threshold to pain is questionable. He had a massive CVA [stroke] 15 years ago and he was given two hours to live. He still likes music, although he can no longer hold the recorder, poetry and plays. At an apt moment he recites lines from a play. His local memory is less accurate.

Total strangers respond to him when he sits outside yet to all appearance he just sits there. [This issue will be looked at in the last two chapters.] Underlying everything he is still anxious, and uncertain of new situations.

Alistair, aged 40, in the workshop

Alistair died aged 50 after becoming increasingly frail and suffering from a deteriorating kidney function. His mum passed away a year later.

His early history (taken from an interview with a doctor when Alistair was aged 10) mentions that he was an only child. His mum felt marvellous during the pregnancy, better than ever since. He was three weeks overdue and his mother had a medical induction. It was a normal birth. He seemed quite all right for the first six months but put on weight slowly, slept a lot and vomited after his feeds. At 6 months he was seen at the children's hospital and a heart defect was diagnosed. Vomiting continued. At 1 year he spent 3 months in the hospital, where he lost 2 pounds, weighing 11 pounds at 15 months. Vomiting continued up to 2½ years, and only then did he start to sit up on his own. Then he improved, started to stand up and could walk by 3 years old. He had then come on to solid foods. Speech had started before he had been sitting up and developed quite well. He went to nursery at age 4 and made good progress. He went to another school for four years where he made little progress. For the first three years he had many characteristics of a typical baby, then he suddenly turned into a little man. Since age 3 he has been clean and dry, and he could dress himself. He didn't like his lessons, was happy and easy to handle, ate quite well now and slept well. The doctor described him as a small but well-developed boy. He had a longish head, bad teeth and ears which were big and a bit unformed. The hands and fingers were beautiful and warm, the feet big and rather flat and broad. He had a congenital heart murmur. He talked incessantly with a good and very large vocabulary, and was very polite and charming. He could not draw or write anything.

The question is, therefore, whether Alistair's early development really was normal. Most Williams Syndrome children fail to thrive in infancy and have digestive and sleeping problems; they also tend to show initial serious delay in their language development.

It is known that in 97 per cent of cases of Williams Syndrome, there is a small piece of Chromosome 7 missing, namely q11 to q23. This causes a disruption in the elastine gene, which is an important gene in the formation of connective tissue. This is one of the 20 genes mutated in Williams Syndrome. The heart abnormality characteristics of this syndrome (narrowing of the aorta) can also be explained through a disturbance of the elastine gene. We know that some 20 genes are deleted and scientists are still searching for an explanation of the behavioural phenotype.

Neuroanatomy

Neuroanatomy is the study of the anatomical structure of the brain. Most scientists in this field in early studies used to concentrate their research on the neuroanatomy of the syndrome; now they are concentrating on brain function rather than structure. Particularly interesting for me is the research of Jernigan and Bellugi in 1990 (cited in Harris 1995). They compared the neuroanatomical structure of people with Down Syndrome with that of people with Williams Syndrome. They found a polarity comparable to that mentioned earlier by von Arnim and Engel (1964). The research was done using Magnetic Resonance Imaging (MRI). During MRI, with the help of a magnetic field, a representation is made of the brain. There is a strong tendency nowadays to see the brain as a computer, as a piece of hardware. Some scientists try to explain the origin of all human behaviour as seated in the brain. This is not my opinion. It is clear to me that you can be limited or helped by certain genetically determined brain structures but in the end what really matters is your own personality.

To come back to the brain structure as shown under MRI: people with Down Syndrome and Williams Syndrome have a smaller brain than average – about 80 per cent of the average brain size. People with Down Syndrome also have a clearly smaller cerebellum. In contrast, people with Williams Syndrome have a relatively large cerebellum and brainstem. In general the cerebrum of people with Williams Syndrome is on the small side but that does not apply to the whole cerebrum. The frontal lobe and some parts of the temporal lobe are selectively well developed. It is known that the temporal lobe is related to linguistic abilities. Neurologists are very interested in this because it could explain the relative language ability of people with Williams Syndrome, and also their musicality and social gifts. (Although scientists are now aware that the musicality of people with Williams Syndrome is not more pronounced than the feeling for music in people with Down Syndrome.) People with Down Syndrome have a different brain map: the frontal cortex is relatively small with a normally developed sub-cortex.

To help us better understand the special qualities of a person with a syndrome, it is useful to look at people with a polar constitution. 'Polar' is not the same as 'opposite': a polarity is a dynamic state – a person can be at any point on a polarity, and may move along it in either direction. For instance, a well-known polarity is male/female, and increasingly in our culture men are trying to be caring and develop their emotional life ('female' qualities) while women are becoming more assertive (a 'male' attribute). I propose that Down and Williams Syndromes are polar conditions, and in understanding one

Table 6.1

Down Syndrome	Williams Syndrome
Learning disability (from mild to severe)	Learning disability (from mild to severe)
Chromosome abnormality: Trisomy 21	Deletion on Chromosome 7
Usually not inherited	Not inherited
1: 600/700 live births	1: 20,000 live births
Speech relatively underdeveloped	Speech relatively well developed
Often reduced hearing	Oversensitive to sounds
Lives in the moment	Anxious about future
Trusts in life	Anxious generally
Relatively good spatial awareness	Poor spatial awareness
Slow facial recognition	Quick facial recognition
Mostly smooth hair	Curly hair
Thick, often rough skin	Thin, tight skin
Frequent congenital heart abnormality with open connection between two sides of heart	Often congenital heart abnormality, stenotic
Eyes fall slightly away in face	Open, sparkly eyes
Cerebrum 80% of average size	Cerebrum 80% of average size
Cerebellum smaller	Cerebellum normal
Frontal cortex smaller	Frontal cortex normal
Temporal cortex smaller	Temporal cortex average size
Subcortex normal size	Subcortex smaller
Musical, difficulty in keeping tune	Very musical

syndrome it can help to explore the experience of a person with another syndrome. Table 6.1 shows the similarities and differences between these two conditions.

'Cocktail-party' speech?

I read a newspaper article in which a mother related her experiences of how she took her young daughter, who had a slight heart murmur, to a cardiac specialist. The daughter greeted the doctor and his two assistants in her usual enthusiastic manner, to which the doctor responded with an all-knowing glance towards his students. 'Typical "cocktail-party" speech,' he beamed. Almost glowing with self-satisfaction, he gave the mother the diagnosis – Williams Syndrome – unaware of the devastating effect it had on her. (People with Williams Syndrome don't have 'cocktail-party' speech – their speech is far more meaningful. They may have a 'cocktail-party' style – social use of language with an outgoing, chatty manner – but they make sense and carry thoughts through.) The mother, totally dazed, went to have a drink with her daughter in a café. There she struck up a conversation with the man at the next table because she had to unburden herself. It turned out that he worked with children with a learning disability and he said to her: 'IQ is not the only way of measuring intelligence. Each child with special needs is an individual with their own unique gifts and qualities.'

The mother ended the article with the words: 'Who needs social skill training here, my daughter or the consultant?'

Complementary treatments

It is not the aim of this book to write down clever thoughts about people with a syndrome. The hope is that the true understanding of how it is to live with a particular syndrome will help us to support people even better.

One specific way I, as a complementary trained doctor, have been doing this is by giving potentized (diluted and rhythmically shaken) remedies. But how do I know what to give?

Down Syndrome and silica supplements

A complementary treatment which may be beneficial is a dietary supplement. How do I choose what process to use? I often give children with Down Syndrome a substance made of silica, that is rhythmically potentized. If we give silica we stimulate clarity, structure and lightness. Think of the beautifully formed structure of a mountain crystal. People with Down Syndrome often lack this clarity and form. Then I think about the purulent mucus which runs from the nose in many children with Down Syndrome and you get a polar picture of the clarity of the crystal. The reduced hearing because of liquid behind the ear and the regular fungal skin infections, especially of feet and toenails, is another frequent problem for children with Down Syndrome which points to the same treatment. Giving the clarity of silica can help a child to create her own clarity.

As I discussed in Chapter 5, the ability to be intellectual and think clearly is not the strongest point of people with Down Syndrome. They respond from their human warmth and emotions. By giving potentized silica you stimulate the body to create silica quality in itself. Silica is an important part of a nutritious diet and is found in grains – wheat, corn and barley, for instance. Problems will arise when the diet is deficient in silica. The story of Marie made this clear to me.

Marie is a young woman with Down Syndrome. From a distance she seems frail and slow, she is very hypotonic and shuffles. On meeting her you quickly realize that the first impression was false. She is a clear thinker, sparkly and funny, and can be extremely stubborn. She suffered her whole life from severe chewing and swallowing problems and lived on purified food. As a young child she suffered from many infections and was successfully put on a dairy-free diet. Her diet was limited, consisting only of soya products, prunes, carrots and chicken, and lacking sufficient silica.

Slowly we adjusted her diet and added fine wheat flour, corn flour or bakery flour to her diet. She made enormous progress. She managed to negotiate the stairs, cycle a tricycle and looked better. 'Yes,' admitted her mum, 'her feet first appeared like lumps of flesh, now they have a form, you can see they are feet.' Silica surely helped in this process.

Williams Syndrome and calcium

Which substance would be helpful if I wanted to support a person with Williams Syndrome? I would choose calcium. In order to have more insight into the role calcium plays I studied Kent's *Materia Medica* (Kent 1946), a classical handbook for homeopathy. According to Kent's description, a typical patient in need of calcium carbonicum has great intellectual disability, the teeth are poorly developed or don't come through, the patient is a late walker as a child and is often full of anxiety and worries. The description continues in the book, but relates more to physical illness.

The potentized remedy calcium carbonicum is made out of oyster shells. The oyster is a special animal; it separates calcium to create a hard external protection around its vulnerable, slimy body and sticks itself to the bottom of the sea. People with Williams Syndrome are too open, don't feel sufficiently guarded and are not able to protect themselves against loud noises or the insecurity of the future. Potentized oyster shell can give an organism an example of how to relate in a positive way to the encapsulating quality of calcium. Calcium and silica create an interesting polarity. Silica helps the organism to become permeable, open to influences of the outside world. Calcium helps to create a sheath or an outer house.

These thoughts demonstrate how as a doctor I try to find the right remedy. It is quite possible for somebody with Down Syndrome to need calcium, perhaps, instead of silica. Readers with a homoeopathic background will have noticed that my way of approaching the remedies contradicts Hahneman's (the founder of homeopathy) rule: you give the same for the same.

CHAPTER SEVEN

Rubenstein-Taybi Syndrome

Mari is visiting the school where I work to see if it is the right place for her. Mari is 16 years old, small of stature. She makes a somewhat square impression with her stiff limbs; her speech is clear but slow, without any melody. Her middle face seems flat with a prominent Roman nose. She has moderate developmental problems, but no reason has ever been found for this. I am left with the feeling that she probably has a genetic syndrome of some kind. As I look at her photograph, it occurs to me: she clearly resembles the 'twins'. These are two young women, well known to me, who have Rubenstein-Taybi Syndrome.

History

This syndrome was first described in 1963 by Rubenstein and Taybi. As such it is quite rare and occurs in only 1 in 100,000 births (nevertheless, I know five people with this condition and the remarkable fact is that their names are fairly similar; they often start with a 'c' and all have many 'a' sounds in their name). An alternative name for this syndrome is 'large thumb and large toe syndrome'. The large thumb and/or large toe are one of the most common characteristics.

The twins

The twins are most clear in my mind, identical twins with the same syndrome. I still find it difficult not to confuse them, they are so identical. Still, they have clearly different personalities, each with their own inner world. Sandra was born first after a pregnancy of 38 weeks. The birth was induced and there were no complications. She weighed 5 lb and spent two weeks in an incubator. As such, she was responding well, but her motor development was delayed. She sat at 18 months and spoke at 3 years. Words started at the age of 4, the age at which she and her sister Lucy started school. During the daytime she was dry but needed a nappy at night. She cried a lot, was quite hyperactive and was on the go the whole time. She was quicker than her sister with her development. At the age of 3, a heart operation was required to close the congenital heart defect. She spent the rest of her school years in the residential school. At one point she and her sister lived in different houses to stimulate their independent development. The story goes that sometimes they swapped places on purpose and it could take some time before the group leader noticed she had the wrong girl. Lucy looks very similar to Sandra and has the same abilities, but she relates differently to the world and is more easygoing than Sandra.

Sandra and her twin sister

At the age of 18, they both moved to a training centre for young people with special needs. Life was not easy for Sandra at that point, because 18 is an age at which a young adult starts to find his or her own life path. This is tough enough for any youngster, let alone for those with extra problems. It can be a crisis point for people with special needs. This period was especially difficult for Sandra because the contact with her own family ceased. Sandra could be aggressive and difficult for her carers and she pulled people's hair. She was very much supported at this time by intensive counselling. Gradually during the sessions she managed to develop some insight into her own behaviour. She was not able to transfer this insight into daily life right away and could still be difficult for some time. During the sessions she used her counsellor as her conscience. Slowly she relaxed and felt more at ease in daily life. She has a great interest in and warmth for people around her. After two years, the counselling was stopped as she had started to discuss more general issues and her life was more in balance. She even had a positive visit from her mother. During this time she also worked with art therapy, working with colours in order to create a certain harmony in her painting. This supported her in working through her inner emotional turmoil. She is still an outgoing lady with a strong emotional life, but her overwhelming feelings can, for example, prevent her from going shopping independently. When writing this chapter I wrote to the carer of Sandra to see how she was getting on. I will quote from the letter of the carer:

> I read your chapter to Sandra. She was very happy with this. It was interesting that as I read (very slowly and calmly) she became quite excited to hear about herself and couldn't keep her hands still, touching me lightly all the time. I find it strange that she doesn't respond to peace and stillness in another person and that she seems happiest when she has stirred up the environment to her own pace. She does this all the time when she is out and because of her friendly outgoing nature often succeeds in getting the reaction she seeks. It is almost as though she vibrates at a higher velocity than the rest of the world and

tries her environment to suit her. As you can imagine this can be upsetting for other residents and there are many resulting battles.

The following are Sandra's own words:

> I like learning to write my own name. I enjoy outings – going to the cinema and restaurants. I like visiting my Mum and Dad. I work on the farm in Corbenic [a Camphill place for adults] with the chickens, goats and donkeys. I also like making cakes and biscuits in the confectionary. I like being happy and love living in Corbenic. It is good to make new friends. I sometimes get into bad moods. Yesterday I was drying the dishes and I lost my temper and I hit Ben. I said sorry afterwards. I like discos and shopping. I love my sister Lucy. I get upset if people give me a row.

Description

Bodily features

Rubenstein-Taybi children are quite easily recognizable. The eyes are wide apart, the eyelids can droop and the eyelashes are long. Often the children wear glasses because of visual problems. The nose is quite prominent and is beaked or straight. The mouth is small with a high arched palate and because of this the teeth are often crowded. The form of the thumb and big toe is obviously different – they are broad and often a bit outstanding.

Growth and development

Children with Rubenstein-Taybi Syndrome weigh 2.5 kg or less at birth, grow slowly and are small. During infancy, there can often be feeding difficulties. There is a general developmental delay. The microcephaly (small head) is an indication of the slow growth of the brain. Congenital heart abnormalities are fairly common as in Sandra's case; there can also be problems with the urinary tract. They can often have fungal nail infections. There is a tendency to have keloid (raised flesh) formation after a wound. The EEG shows an unusual brain wave pattern in 66 per cent of the children, but only 25 per cent have epilepsy. The life span is normal.

Behaviour – soul life

Not only are there many similarities in their physical features and development, but also there are many similarities in the behaviour of the children and adults with this condition. Most have quite a poor concentration span and are easily distracted. They are better in activities than in verbal skills. They are generally perceived as outgoing with a happy disposition and are easily sociable; they are too friendly and love adult attention. They respond well to music. Most will become independent in their self-care activities. When you see people with this condition walk you will observe a certain stiffness, lack of natural flow in their movements. The fine motor skills are especially affected because of the way the thumb is formed. Half of the children have self-stimulating behaviour, like clapping hands, rocking and turning around. Most children dislike a change of environment. They are often over-sensitive to noise. Adults with this syndrome can have sudden mood changes with stroppy moods.

Expression of personality

Speech development can be difficult and some children do not develop any speech at all, but they will use their language effectively and positively and there is a good grasp of language. Speech is mostly good and understandable, although it can be quite fast. The mild to moderate learning disability will mean that people with this syndrome need support during their lives, in their living situation and at work.

Cause and scientific background

This is quite a rare syndrome – just over 600 people are recognized as having Rubenstein-Taybi worldwide. The cause is not totally clear. What is clear is that there is a genetic background to it and the fact that identical twins can have the syndrome is a proof of this; it can occur in families, but usually only one member has the condition. Recent research finds in some people small genetic changes, mainly in Chromosome 16.

Discussion

In general people with this condition are outgoing and open. This can come across as a lack of distance to other people, as they are very sociable and love company. In general, their intellectual capacity is moderate. They respond very directly to the world, are very open, but a certain fear can be hidden behind this. If their behaviour becomes challenging, it is often related to their feeling overwhelmed by the surrounding world. In my experience, there can be a lack of flexibility in the reaction to the environment, and some obsessional elements can be present. There are, of course, some limitations in the taking control of their own life, as the finer and gross motor skills, especially the grasp of the special thumb, being affected. Their main way of relating to the world is emotional, and this can sometimes be upsetting. A different way of trying to empathize with people with Rubenstein-Taybi Syndrome is to look at polarities. We all know people who are more introvert while others are extrovert. People with this condition are mostly extrovert and are sometimes in danger of losing their sense of self.

Approach

Individualized help is important. In general, people with Rubenstein-Taybi Syndrome will need help to develop and find their own inner centre. Speech therapy can be important and education has to take any special educational needs into account. Counselling was very helpful for Sandra to deal with her problems and to find her own centre. Her stay here also illustrated how important it is to try to understand individuals through their own life story. It can also be helpful to know that the syndrome coloured the way her inner struggles were expressed.

CHAPTER EIGHT

Fragile X Syndrome
A Constitutional Threshold Experience

Every month I visit a small residential school for children with special needs. This time a new boy has arrived. He is sitting in the entrance hall, unable to join the rest of the school. After observing him for two minutes, I ask the person in charge whether he has Fragile X Syndrome. His large head and outstanding ears, but more than this his habit of avoiding eye contact, make this very obvious to me.

It has been known for a long time that developmental problems are more common amongst men than women. Langdon Down, the first person to describe Down Syndrome, made this discovery as early as 1866 during research on 2000 children in which he found a ratio of 2.1: 0.9 between boys and girls (Harris 1995). Later, an explanation was found in the fact that certain genetic syndromes are related to the X chromosome. Men will present the inherited problem, having only one X chromosome, while women will act as carriers of the affected chromosome.

History

Fragile X Syndrome was first recognized in 1943. It is the second most common cause of learning disability, Down Syndrome being the most common. It is found all over the world and in all races. The incidence is 1 in 4–6000 men and 1 in 8000 women, although recent research questions these figures, suggesting a lower incidence rate.

The main difference with Down Syndrome is that Fragile X occurs in certain families and is inherited.

Around 80 per cent of men with this syndrome have a learning disability. Amongst women this rate is 39 per cent. Another 33 per cent of the women have a specific learning disability. So, this condition is not only present in males with their one X chromosome. There are also women with this syndrome who will have a healthy X chromosome next to their Fragile X chromosome.

Fragile X Syndrome was discovered in 1969 by Herbert Lubs, who showed that just a small part of a gene on the X chromosome is unstable. In 1991 it became clearer that there is quite a spectrum of presentation: some people are hardly affected while others have a clear learning disability. It was also in 1991 that Verkerk found the specific gene that relates to Fragile X Syndrome. This gene is situated on the X chromosome and contains a repetitive sequence known as CGG (cytosine guanine guanine). This sequence is normally repeated around 30 times, but it can happen that it is repeated too often. The carrier range begins at around 50 repeats and can reach as many as 200 repeats. The carrier will have hardly any problems, but it can happen that this unstable part of the gene multiplies itself further during the meiosis (separation) of the female egg cell. If the CGG repeat is present more than two hundred times, a part of the X chromosome is silenced (this is called FMR–1 gen) and the syndrome presents itself.

To sum up we can say:

- The syndrome occurs in certain families.
- There is a relationship with the X chromosome.
- If a male carrier has a daughter, she will also be a carrier.
- A child of a female carrier can receive the full mutation and the syndrome becomes visible.
- The symptoms are usually less pronounced in women than in men.

So, a mother who is a carrier has a 50 per cent chance of passing on the gene related to this condition. But whether the child is male or female, or has a premutation or full mutation, will affect the outcome. So when a mother passes on her Fragile X gene to her child, the child may be a carrier or may be affected by Fragile X Syndrome. In fact, I talked recently to a mother of three such sons. The first was a bit slow in development. Maybe he is just lazy, she thought. School was also not without its problems for the second son, but it wasn't till the youngest son's problems were investigated that it was clear why all 3 boys had problems – they all had Fragile X Syndrome.

To be a carrier can create heart-searching questions. Is prenatal diagnosis necessary? Should an affected foetus be aborted only when it is a boy? Do I want to conceive any children at all? The Fragile X Society's newsletter has some quite moving stories about those difficult questions carriers face.

Typical behaviour

All these facts raise questions. What type of syndrome is this? Why is it so little known when it is relatively common?

The knowledge concerning this syndrome is quite new. In Scotland I met a young man whose face seemed quite familiar. It was almost shocking how similar he was to a young man who used to live in my house community in Holland – the same physical build, the same way of speaking, even the same way he scratched his head when shy. And they had the same name! Suddenly I realized that the friendly and very sensitive young man from Holland must have had the same syndrome.

The hypersensitivity strikes me as the most characteristic feature. This is apparent at the first meeting – the avoidance of gaze, even the whole head is sometimes turned away. Sometimes the face will be covered with the hands. The way of speaking is typical – they repeat themselves and speak in staccato without properly finishing the sentence. This is certainly not autistic behaviour. An autistic child doesn't look at you and doesn't acknowledge your existence, but it is different for a person with Fragile X Syndrome, who often has a very strong impression of other people. This can be so strong that he can feel overwhelmed by the experience, will withdraw into himself and have to avert his gaze from the other person. Research confirms this.

The speech of people with Fragile X is not meaningless. The repetitions and echolalia are the specific way that they communicate. It is of course quite possible for people with Fragile X Syndrome to have autism, but this would be a very small percentage.

Physical description

Especially after puberty, the men have a large head with a high forehead and an open face, the ears are very visible – large, fleshy and well formed; the eyes have a sparkle to them; they have a wide mouth with firm lips, strong teeth and a prominent jaw. These features are not so typical in women, whose skin is velvety and looks youthful, and who blush easily. Connective tissue dysplasia explains the lax joints, the flat feet and can also cause mitral valve prolapse (a prolapse of the valve on the left side of the heart). In general their stature is smaller than that of the average person. Some can have a squint.

Fertility is normal. The men often have enlarged testicles. Epilepsy can occur in 20 per cent of cases. Hyperactivity can be a common feature, with a short attention span and impulsive character. Outbursts are a real problem; they often happen because something irritates, such as sudden noises, too direct an approach or a general feeling of increasing tension. Two young men I lived with developed tempers when there was lightning and thunder – the charged atmosphere was too much for them.

Recently, I was asked to give a talk to the Fragile X Society and I carried out a survey to see how many people with Fragile X live in the different Camphill communities in Britain and Ireland, which together cater for 1700 people with special needs. According to the response I received, 41 residents had a diagnosis of Fragile X Syndrome and the responders felt that a further 26 people could have Fragile X Syndrome. We know that, especially amongst adults with special needs, there are many people who are not diagnosed. So if I could assume that half of this undiagnosed group had Fragile X Syndrome, then 54 men live with this condition in Camphill – an estimated 3 per cent of residents, which is quite a considerable number. Nobody mentioned any women.

One of the questions in the questionnaire was regarding the quality of the lives of the people with Fragile X Syndrome. The answers varied from 'excellent' and 'very high' to 'high' and 'good'. This was despite the fact that 47 per cent of this group could still have temper tantrums.

Neuroanatomy

Researchers have tried to investigate the brains of people with Fragile X chromosomes. Some parts of the brain are clearly extra developed – this is probably caused by inactivation of gene FMRP which usually harmonizes normal ceil growth. The middle part of the cerebellum – the posterior vermis cerebilli – is quite small. This is the part of the brain which normally works to integrate and harmonize inner and external impressions, and thus its small size could explain the problems these people experience with sensory hypersensitivity, their chaotic motor movements and disorganized use of language – in all of these no unity is reached.

Psychological tests

Tests have taken place to assess the degree of learning disability. Most IQ tests show an IQ of 35–70 (average IQ is 100+) with a relative strength in speech. More limited is the ability to solve problems which follow on from each other; different impressions are very quickly overwhelming. Also characteristic are the difficulty in concentrating, poor short-term memory, dealing with sequences of information and problems with maths and number work.

Even men with this syndrome who have hardly any learning disability still have specific problems in these areas, but they are relatively able in reading, spelling and visually sorting out objects. Out of all women with this syndrome, 50 per cent do not express it and have a normal IQ; the other 50 will have a moderate or mild learning disability. Women have the same problems with mathematics, concentration and poor short-term memory but their strength is verbal expression. Shyness, anxiety and social isolation are not uncommon.

Language

People with Fragile X Syndrome have a characteristic speech pattern. It seems almost as if the language streams through them, instead of them actively talking. Speech development is delayed; sentences are not fluent or finished, echolalia is present and speech is repetitive. Sometimes they get stuck in sentences (verbal perseveration). The pitch can vary and give the impression of the recitation of a litany.

It is quite clear that the speech is special. In general, people with this condition are verbal and communicative, and their verbal expressions are never without meaning or emotional expression, as with a person with autism. They are often quite direct and clear in their relationship to others. If you listen carefully, many observant remarks are present in their cluttered speech. Sometimes this never-ceasing stream of oral comments can become tiring for the listener, however interesting the content.

Threshold experience

Lotte Sahlmann worked as a doctor in Camphill communities in England and described in 1963 a group of young men who had large heads, outstanding ears and soft, easy-blushing skin and were very over-sensitive. She felt that those people had strong feelings of shame, hence they avert their gaze on greeting others. She called them people with 'ego hysteria' (personal communication). By this she meant that such people live with their awareness and personality very much in their surroundings, their personality is around them, not in themselves. The word 'hysteria' can be confusing, as it is used in so many different contexts. As a medical term, 'hysteria' refers to a group of mental disorders where people have a symptom without an illness. This happens unconsciously; for instance, a person suddenly cannot walk. In ordinary language, 'hysteria' means extravagant behaviour. Both descriptions of hysteria point to the fact that something is not in control or is 'loosened'. In the medical definition of 'hysteria', the physical symptoms are not under control. In the everyday use of the word, the emotions are not under control. 'Ego hysteria' points to the fact that the ego – the personality – is not under the control of the person.

Later, in the 1980s, it became clear that 'ego hysteria' referred to the same condition as the scientific term 'Fragile X Syndrome'.

Lotte Sahlmann had a deep connection to many men with Fragile X Syndrome and she described how people with this condition live with a special soul constellation. This soul constellation is very pronounced, but we can all recognize elements of it in ourselves. In our modern-day culture, feelings of fear, restlessness and unease are on the increase. We only have to observe the ever-increasing need for psychotherapy, counselling and other therapies. People who have gone through a therapeutic process are aware how shattering the results of counselling can be: 'You experience yourself as bare and all outer layers of pretence fall away.' During such a therapeutic process people are often not able to function fully in other daily activities, because the therapy requires such an input. People with Fragile X Syndrome are permanently living with this experience; these people, with their vulnerable, silent gene, are constantly aware of their limitations, their one-sidedness and their disability. Not only that but also they are aware of the vulnerable sides of their fellow humans. This is an overwhelming experience that compels them to avert their gaze when meeting with others, and many even become red in the face as if they are full of shame. They live on the threshold of ordinary consciousness, which can be a paralysing experience.

I could observe this clearly with Bart, a tall, strapping young man. Nothing wrong at first glance, except a moderate degree of learning disability. But why couldn't he even manage to wash the kitchen floor? Too direct or rash an approach was so painful for him that he would fly into a temper during which he could hurt people, but when the temper was over he was left full of remorse and shame. His saving grace was that his morality and spiritual life were well developed, which gave him support time and again.

His over-sensitivity made him very aware of his fellow human beings: he was almost clairvoyant regarding other people's emotions. This was easy to observe during all the years I shared a house with him. He could volunteer many sharp remarks and observations, but if his mood was low his language would become rude. He knew that I was in a bad mood even before I would say anything or had even looked at him.

Once Bart met a person he had not met before. I myself knew this man and knew of his inner conflicts and struggles. Within one minute, Bart started to lecture him: 'Who do you think you are, who are you? You are sitting there writing in your room, but that is not the answer.' The man was shocked and amazed. 'Hello,' he said, 'Who is this young man?' The man was confronted with his own doubts. This example clarifies just how directly and intensely people with Fragile X Syndrome can be aware of other people.

This over-sensitivity can make certain aspects of life difficult, like entering a room full of people, or coping with thresholds, going from one space to another. How often did I observe Bart lounging in front of the dining room door, speaking loudly to himself? Sometimes he could manage to enter the dining room, sometimes not. A joke or a hand on the shoulder or a gentle push could help, but not always.

The subtitle of this chapter, 'A constitutional threshold experience', characterizes Joe's situation clearly. Joe was in the same class as my 5-year-old son and had the typical beautiful large head with outstanding ears of someone with Fragile X. Joe was invited to my son's birthday party together with other children in the nursery class. This was an integrated nursery class. Would Joe dare to enter the room? Adult encouragement does not help. The helpful hand of another child seemed to be the best approach and Joe settled happily in a corner and played by himself. Around him the birthday party went on. He also withdrew during the class party to which all the parents were invited; he played contentedly in the Wendy House.

I happened to come across a school report on one of our youngsters with Fragile X Syndrome. It is such a lively and accurate description of the daily life of a person with Fragile X Syndrome that I would like to share it here.

School report

When Ian joined the Camphill schools, he was brought by his mother and two social workers, arriving at lunchtime. The stress of facing such a new situation was clearly too much for him. He took refuge in an armchair, covered his face with his hands and peeped between his fingers when he thought no one was looking. Any effort to make friends with him or to entice him to the table resulted in paroxysms of embarrassment and swearing and only an hour later, when alone with one adult, could he shyly emerge to enjoy his waiting meal.

During the past school year Ian has progressed extremely well. He has made a place for himself in our house where his warm heart and kindly concern are much appreciated.

Ian is now fifteen years old, of average height and with the physique typical for children handicapped by constitutional over-sensitivity. His head is somewhat large and capped by a mass of brown silky curls, his face is broad and open, he has sparkling brown eyes and a wide, rather fleshy mouth which is usually open in a cheerful grin. His body is somewhat unwieldy, his fingers and toes stumpy. His skin is unusually fine and transparent, he blushes easily and in situations of slight stress or insecurity he becomes covered in warm perspiration. His general appearance is one of freshness coupled with extreme sensitivity. Ian can undress himself after a fashion but needs considerable assistance with dressing. Vests, shirts and jumpers he dons inside out or back to front and his shoes are invariably on the wrong feet! He cannot yet fasten buttons or cope with shoelaces and ties. When he is undressing, he drags at his shirt until the buttons 'come undone' or fly off! His clumsy, awkward body hinders him in all finely co-ordinated movements. He likes to be kept clean but cannot of himself decide when to change his clothes.

While Ian is quick to notice any slight untidiness in another, he is generally oblivious to his own appearance; however, when he is dressed up for a special occasion he shows his pleasure in a beaming smile radiating well-being from every pore.

At meal times, Ian can be a strenuous neighbour as he can only eat tidily with frequent reminders. He handles knife and fork somewhat ineptly and needs space to spread himself at the table. He frequently sprawls over his neighbours, reaching over them to pass dishes or to get what he wants himself. He has a hearty appetite with little idea of when to stop. When Ian first arrived he was grossly overweight and became rude or abusive if his diet was controlled, until he had to leave the room. We have worked at this and he now accepts his diet reasonably.

Ian sleeps soundly at night, falling asleep as soon as he is in bed. Until quite recently he wetted his bed each night unless he was lifted during the evening. He was very ashamed of this and naturally quite unable to cope with his laundry. During the past few weeks he has kept dry without lifting, toileting himself proudly in the early morning. By day, Ian still sometimes soils himself in stressful situations; he is helped by reminders to use the toilet and he now requests adult assistance to change or use toilet paper.

Ian can wash himself with some help, he cleans his own teeth but cannot brush his hair effectively or trim his nails. Most of what he does is performed in a slapdash manner, hence the results are generally somewhat sketchy. He is sensitive to pain and has some awareness of hot and cold. He is dependent on our daily routine and structure and now begins to show some reliability in knowing where he should be at a given time. For this he relies on the sequence of events as he is unable to use a watch or tell the time.

Extreme bashfulness makes any direct approach agonizing. When addressed directly he will smile, blush painfully and turn away. His embarrassment can be so great that his whole body wriggles and twists in despair, and he can explode into shouting, swearing or spitting. He is so shy and over-aware of himself that even a critical glance can cause violent outbreaks of howling and swearing! He can cope with a conversation only when one directs one's gaze away from him and at times it is helpful to turn one's whole head in another direction when speaking to him.

These difficulties were evident on his daily ride to join his class. Our van has two rows of facing seats. Ian's vociferous dislike of the van disappeared as soon as he was allowed to sit in front and he now goes off quietly without any fuss. On the whole, Ian is usually friendly and co-operative but if he is approached without regard for his personal feelings, violent outbursts of temper, aggression towards his tormentor and floods of tears can be expected. In the course of the year he has become much calmer and more self-contained and his tantrums are far less frequent.

Ian is extraordinarily talkative. At first, every observation and experience was accompanied by a spate of running commentary which made him too noisy a participant for most of our common gatherings. When restrained from talking he had a repertoire of noises i.e. burping, groaning, wheezing, all of which he used to disturb any quiet moment. In this respect Ian has improved remarkably and it is now rarely necessary to remove him from social gatherings, provided an adult is beside him. Thus, he attends plays, concerts and our weekly or seasonal festivals.

When answering a question, Ian's speech is rambling with a broad Edinburgh accent, either whispered or mumbled in a quick, monotonous way. The more direct the questions or demand, the faster and more incomprehensible his reply. He seldom gives a direct answer, preferring to shoot off at a tangent in his monosyllabic, repetitive replies. On the other hand he often makes quite relevant observations or appropriate remarks about daily events, repeating the same remark three or four times without drawing breath, for instance a yawn or shiver may elicit 'You tired, Avril?' 'You tired?' 'Tired, tired Avril?' or 'You cold, cold Nobo,' or 'You got meetin? Meetin? Meetin?' and so on.

Ian is extremely sociable, he likes to offer his help in making cups of tea or fetching what is needed; in spite of his ungainly clumsiness he can carry full cups or jugs on a tray without spilling them. When praised Ian shows his pleasure by stiffening his body, taking a deep breath and 'flapping his wings' in front of his chest in a paroxysm of delight.

Ian is an observer by nature, his interests are entirely centred around the human affairs concerning those around him. The well-being of others, their whereabouts and doings, is of the utmost importance to him, hence he cannot occupy himself for more than a few minutes without losing interest and gravitating to one of the common rooms to see what is afoot. He likes to stand next to conversations and telephone calls, showing his pleasure by 'flapping his wings'. The building site opposite has acted like a magnet. He was always to be found watching the work, returning to the kitchen for brief visits, to make sure that all was well.

He is an excellent cleaner and given a one-to-one situation with little distraction, he can reliably clean kitchen shelves and drawers. Ian is learning to make his bed and to dry up but his ability is always completely dependent on his mood.

During the past school year Ian has settled down and made good progress. He has been a boisterous warm-hearted member of our group of children, well loved by all. It will be necessary to move Ian to another house next autumn; we hope that the change will not upset him and we look forward to watching his further progress.

(Housemother)

How is Ian progressing? Has he managed to live with his syndrome? One thing is certain – he always manages to meet people who really like him and support him. He finished school and later went to a training centre for young adults where his outbursts became less frequent, but when they did occur they were quite noticeable – three men would be required to prevent him causing harm, and he required

Ian, aged 25

two days' rest to recover from such an outburst. After ten years in the training centre, Ian was ready to move on, but it was not easy to find a new place for him. People were a bit apprehensive when they heard about his potential outbursts. In the end, he went home. This was not an ideal solution, as his family could not really look after him. However, he again managed to find people who were committed to him and he now lives in another small farm-based Camphill placement.

Support

How can we help these people? As children they are often accused of being lazy, but I hope it is now clear where the difficulties in engagement come from. My experience is that it is most important to respect their over-sensitivity.

An indirect approach with a clear structure is helpful; be aware that their personality is around them, and address them accordingly. They will also respond well when a group of involved people meet without their presence and create a common understanding, attitude and resolve. They will sense this and respect it. The approach in school depends, of course, on the degree of learning disability and on any specific problem, e.g. dyslexia.

Very often, people with Fragile X Syndrome are open and interested in other people.

In the questionnaire to all the Camphill communities that I mentioned earlier, it was remarked that the adults did very well in rural village communities. There they meet not only structure but also freedom. Often they also like to work in village stores, where their awareness of the different customers is very helpful. Therapeutic support can be helpful, in the form of artistic therapy. Sometimes I had to give some allopathic medication to help the person to be more relaxed and less over-sensitive. Complementary remedies can also be helpful.

For specific help, the Fragile X Society has a wealth of information.

Summary

The typical characteristics change with age.

As young children:

- avoid eye contact
- play close to their peers, but not with them
- frequently repeat their own words
- react negatively to authority
- develop late
- have a special temperament (lack of concentration, overactive, impulsive).

After puberty:

- learning disabilities
- typical facial features
- enlarged testicles
- relatively good memory but poor arithmetic.

CHAPTER NINE

Foetal Alcohol Syndrome

In the local village are 20 shops. You will be hard pressed to find underwear or shoelaces in any of them, but it is easy to buy alcohol. Two large shops are full of it, and it is available in the local supermarket in all forms and strengths. Alcohol is very much part of our culture. This chapter discusses the effect of alcohol on the unborn child and the consequences this can have. Foetal Alcohol Syndrome is, of course, not a genetically determined syndrome. I include it in this book because, in my work as a doctor, I encounter many children with this condition.

Worldwide, Foetal Alcohol Syndrome is a common cause of physical and psychological developmental problems. International studies mention an incidence of 19 in every 10,000 children who are severely affected, and 1 in every 300 children who are moderately affected.

History

The use, or misuse, of alcohol during pregnancy is mentioned in the Old Testament, in Judges, Chapter 13, Verse 4: 'Therefore beware, and drink no wine or strong drink, and eat nothing unclean.'

Aristotle, a Greek philosopher who lived from 384BC to 322BC stated: 'Silly, drunk women with hare brains often bring children in the world who resemble them.' Already, during Aristotle's life, it was recognized that children from alcoholic mothers appeared dull and missed the playfulness or joy of life. Between 1720 and 1750, a so-called gin epidemic happened in England. Many people drank large quantities of gin. Doctors noticed that an abundant use of alcohol by the mother had a poor influence on their children. By the end of the nineteenth century there were descriptions of the negative effects of alcohol on the unborn child.

Therefore it is quite shocking to realize that it was only in 1970 that Foetal Alcohol Syndrome was 'discovered' (Harris 1995). Since 1970 there has been a growing awareness of the negative influence of alcohol on adults. The British government has guidelines for a sensible consumption of alcohol: 21 units per week for women and 28 units per week for men. Moderate alcohol use has, of course, also a known positive effect on health, and moderate alcohol drinkers experience some protection against cardiovascular diseases. However, the awareness of the effect of alcohol on the unborn baby is still quite limited.

Early damage

Alcohol can damage the embryo as early as the first few weeks of pregnancy, before the woman even knows that she is pregnant. While 21 units of alcohol may be a good guideline for an adult woman, it poses quite a risk for her unborn baby, especially if a large amount of alcohol is consumed during binge drinking.

Research on 31,604 pregnant women showed that even the consumption of one or two glasses of alcohol a day increases the risk of prenatal growth retardation. Some doctors advise women to abstain from alcohol. Advertisements for smoking already carry a warning that it can damage the unborn child. Voices are raised to extend this warning to alcohol advertisements. Mothers seem to know the negative effects, as maybe this story illustrates:

> I was at the hairdresser's and the woman next to me had a loud and lively voice. I couldn't help overhearing her conversation. She was telling about the difficult delivery of her first baby because the baby had been quite big. 'Now,' said she, 'during my next pregnancy I will smoke and drink, and surely then the baby will be smaller.'

Was she kidding?

Description

These children can be affected in many different ways. Foetal Alcohol Syndrome is diagnosed when there is alcohol abuse during pregnancy and the children have the following characteristics after birth:

- Growth deficiency, which starts before birth and continues after birth.

- Central nervous system involvement, with signs of neurological and developmental problems and/or behavioural abnormalities coupled with an intellectual disability; what you see are irritable babies and hyperactive children.

Characteristic facial features occur, with at least two of the following:

- Microcephaly (a too-small head).

- Microophthalmia (too-small eyes) with too-short palpebral fissures.

- Poorly developed phyltrum (lines between nose and mouth), thin upper lip and flattened profile of maxilla (upper jaw).

Therefore, the facial features are underdeveloped. The children can also be affected by other congenital abnormalities and often the heart or skeleton is affected. A great tragedy is hidden in this list of symptoms.

Two different diagnoses can be made. Foetal Alcohol Syndrome (FAS) is reserved for the children who have all the characteristics. Foetal Alcohol Effect (FAE) applies to those children who have some of the problems; these children are not easily recognizable and you have to be knowledgeable to diagnose it.

David

David has the classical syndrome. He is the youngest of four children. His mother was 25 years old at his birth. Both parents were of low intelligence. They both had a drinking problem and the mother was drunk during labour. David was small at birth, weighing 2.29 kg. He began to shake as he experienced alcohol withdrawal symptoms. He went to foster parents when he was 10 days old. He was thought to be a bright child because of early language development and was adopted aged 16 months. He walked at the age of 2 and was toilet trained by 2½. His behaviour became more difficult when he was 4 to 5 years old. He was very restless, showed a lack of concentration and made unduly easy contact with strangers. He would wander away from his parents, quite unafraid of getting lost. By the age of 8 he had gone through four standard schools and both his adoptive parents and the social services recognized that he could not be managed at

David, aged 10

home. He became a pupil at our residential school for children with special needs. This was a painful decision for his parents. His adoptive mother recalled her pain when David didn't show any sign of shyness or homesickness when he was at one point temporarily placed in a foster family.

At the age of 8 he is just 1.25 metres tall and has a small head with the typical features of a child with Foetal Alcohol Syndrome. He is very myopic and wears thick glasses. He appears at first impression an open, lively child with red curly hair. However, it soon became clear what a challenge, for David and his educators, was hidden behind this mask. He was restless, changeable and aggressive and couldn't be part of the small therapeutic class with a high staff to pupil ratio.

How to understand this syndrome

To understand better the effects of alcohol on David we tried to look at different aspects of his being.

Physical body and congenital abnormalities

David is short with a small head and wears strong glasses. All these aspects together with his facial features lead to a recognition of Foetal Alcohol Syndrome. Luckily, he doesn't suffer from epilepsy or congenital deformities.

Vitality and possibilities for outer and inner growth

This is an area which is problematic for David. Not only is his physical growth retarded, but also he has difficulties with inner growth. He seems to have a specific difficulty in learning from past experiences: a mistake can be repeated over and over again. His poor memory, a common problem for these children, is partly the cause of this problem.

His morality is affected by a poor memory. If he does something that is morally wrong, even if he is addressed regarding it, he will do it again, not having internalized the connection.

Soul life

By 'soul life' I mean all aspects of our feelings, our ability to think and our ability to act and plan. David had many behavioural problems, which are characteristic of children with this condition. Another feature is a lack of shyness towards strangers. When David first joined our school he had difficulties with forming emotional attachments. He was restless, had poor concentration levels and could be especially destructive. Suddenly he would run off to hide himself or he would chatter non-stop and could continue asking questions. Reading was quite good but mathematics was a problem. He clearly presented a degree of learning disability. It was clear that his soul life was chaotic, not differentiated and not structured by his personality.

Personality

David appears friendly, warm and outgoing on first encounter. It soon becomes clear that this is more a consequence of his syndrome than of his true personality. (His true or higher personality was never damaged or disabled.) The superficial friendliness masks the severity of his syndrome. David has to imitate his surroundings, the people and him. He really needs one-to-one attention in order to be contained and secure. It seems almost as if, instead of David, we meet a pseudo-personality created by alcohol (if you think of people who are slightly drunk, they are outgoing, appear sociable and friendly). In fact David is an anxious boy, afraid to be left alone.

'The handicapped smile'

Valerie Sinason uses the term 'the handicapped smile' in her book *Mental Handicap and the Human Condition* (1992). She is a psychotherapist who works with children with moderate to severe learning disabilities. She noticed that many children use the smile as a way of surviving; as a mask to hide the inner pain and the feeling of rejection. Many people are not too charmed by people with learning disabilities. The ice breaks if the children are sweet or smile or, as in some cases, clown around.

The smile as a way of surviving was quite clear in David's case. How many traumas does he carry around? We cannot imagine a more severe degree of neglect during pregnancy than that of the perpetual drunkenness of his mother. David's mother gave him up after birth. At 16 months he had to leave his foster parents and life was not so easy with his adoptive parents. He wasn't the intelligent child they had expected, life was difficult with him and he was rejected by three schools before the age of 8. How does a young child cope with all this? A smile can be quite a good protection. In the case of children with syndromes, it is good to ask ourselves: What kind of secondary handicap do they have? How many traumatic situations have they encountered?

The art therapist worked very intensely with David. To start with, he just managed to paint for 10 minutes, a few quick brush strokes, then finished. He couldn't concentrate on an image; there was no fantasy, no inner images. Now, two years later, he can concentrate for 40 minutes during an art therapy session and can create rich images. He recently painted a beautiful Indian – this therapy allowed him to create some balance in his turbulent emotional life and allowed his real individuality to be engaged.

Not long ago I watched him during a play that his class were performing. He played Columbus, who was sailing to America. All his men were in mutiny and refused to sail any further. Now Columbus had to be strict and keep order among his crew. David played well; how strengthening such a play is for his sense of self-worth.

I had a talk with him to see what he would think about his story being included in the book. He thought that would be great. I also asked him to tell me about his life now. He had just turned 16 and still lived in the same school.

> Life is great now. I want to live independent[ly] later, in key housing but have to see what my parents think. I am already independent, going to school alone, shopping in the local village and borrowing CDs from the library. I am not yet going alone to town. Money and time is still difficult. Don't like maths, hate it. Love English; like putting cities of the world in alphabetical

order. Like computer work, that is good. Breakfast cooking [for 20 people!] was difficult to start, but now it works well. Cook breakfast on my own on Monday and Friday, cook porridge, put the spreads at the table, wash the pots, milk in the jugs, porridge in the oven.

Get on fine with other people, sometimes difficult with one other youngster, but we make it up.

I asked him about his tablets – we had tried to stop them six months previously and I was wondering what he thought about that:

I am still taking tablets, it is to help me to calm down. When I stopped for a while I was not myself, totally out of myself. I am much better now.

We are raising money for the homeless now with our class. We had a Ceiligh and will have still a Nicolas Café.

I am trying if I can see my brother and sisters again, but I am not sure if it will work. I don't know if they know that I exist. I have a photo of them. I am not on it. I have never seen my father and mother [he makes it clear that he means here his natural father and mother].

Everything is fine at home, with my father and mother [his adoptive parents].

It is clear that David has done very well. Making steps in independence, mastering new skills, like making breakfast for a big crowd which is not easy, and being concerned for people who are worse off then him.

His wish to find his birth family comes from him, and it is a sensitive issue. But now he has the strength to tackle it.

I have to confess that he also greatly benefited from the drug Carbamazepine (Tegretol), an anti-epileptic which can stabilize mood. This enabled him to be more in control of unconscious mood swings.

Approach

It became very clear to us how deeply David was affected by this syndrome, in all aspects of his being.

How did we help him?

The first and very important step we made was to create a protective layer around him and take all responsibility away from him for his negative behaviour (you can imagine how many negative remarks such a hyperactive, uncontrolled child will meet in a day). It was very important that there was a good co-operation between all carers. David was also quite dependent on the presence of an experienced carer. When it became too much for one carer then a colleague would quietly take over. This protection was also offered in a physically visible way – we made a veil around his bed, creating a really homely place to sleep. A copy of a Madonna painting hung above his bed. This Madonna radiated motherly warmth and safety (the Madonnas painted by Raphael have this special quality).

We told David many fairy tales and later mythological stories, to nourish his inner life. At first it was not possible for him to attend school but he was taught in an individualized programme.

Initially he needed daily massage to strengthen the feeling of protection and peace. Different etheric oils were used – St John's oil or lavender oil. Horse-riding proved extremely helpful as a therapy to practise control and develop his poor sense of balance. During eurythmy therapy (a form of therapy through movement) we stimulated his co-ordination and concentration. All these intense therapeutic activities helped him to engage in his own healing process.

Slowly he could be integrated into his class and after two years was ready for formal learning. I have already mentioned that his reading ability is greater than his maths ability; this is typical for children with Foetal Alcohol Syndrome and probably relates to poor co-ordination. The most important step was David's growing ability to relate to his carers and to his adoptive parents. His mother told me that one day he had to leave for his residential school and when she entered the bathroom she found a message on the steamed-up mirror: 'I love you, Mama.' In all these opportunities to create real relationships we finally encountered David, not his pseudo-personality. Most important has been his courage to work on his problems.

What inner attitude is required for us to work successfully with a child with Foetal Alcohol Syndrome? Such a child requires openness, the opportunity to start every day anew, to leave the mistakes from yesterday behind and be met with an open mind – a real exercise in forgiveness. Older children need strong, clear structures and they will have to experience the consequences of their actions.

Children with Foetal Alcohol Effect

Some children prove to be challenging in their behaviour. These are the children who can be manipulative, changeable and aggressive on occasion – a real challenge for their carers. They often come from a disruptive background where excessive alcohol use by the mother was known to be a real problem. Often these children have mild features of the syndrome; sometimes it is just their head that is smaller than normal.

The knowledge that they are affected by alcohol helps. It explains why they don't make easy progress, and make the same mistake over and over again. It helps us to have more realistic expectations of these youngsters.

Adults with Foetal Alcohol Syndrome

Unfortunately it is not just children who have this condition. The problem is perpetuated into teenage years and adulthood. The developmental problems and behavioural problems especially pose quite a hindrance to independence. Somebody described it once like this: 'Living together with somebody with Foetal Alcohol Syndrome has many similarities to living with a drunkard. Sometimes it is a good drunk, sometimes a nasty drunk but it is still a drunkard.'

The effect of alcohol

Why can alcohol be so damaging to the unborn child? According to Dr Beattie, a paediatrician in Stirling, Scotland, three elements are important:

- Alcohol spreads itself through the bodily fluids to the whole body. The higher the concentration of fluid in an area of the body, the higher the concentration of alcohol. The foetal brain contains a relatively large amount of water, so the concentration of alcohol will also be relatively high.

- The blood from the maternal placenta flows directly towards the foetal brain, bypassing other organs, so the promulgation of the foetal blood is the same as the mother's.

- During foetal development, the liver is not yet able to produce enzymes to break down alcohol (Beattie 19??).

So, if a mother drinks, the foetus will have the same level of alcohol in its blood, especially concentrated in the developing brain; the foetus has even less ability than the mother to break it down. So the alcohol really inhibits the growth of the new cells in the brain.

Alcohol abuse during pregnancy presents a burden for the unborn child. Other drugs used during pregnancy also cause problems. Research in 1989 in America showed that 10 per cent of the subjects had used one or other drugs during pregnancy (Harris 1995).

If the mother is addicted, how do we perceive her freedom, or her ability to change her actions? These are all questions which relate to our society, and this will not go away with the increased use of 'recreational drugs' and drug addiction. We will surely see more new 'syndromes'.

Alcohol use and the father

What are the effects if the father is an alcoholic? Langdon Down wrote in 1887 of his conviction of the relationship between paternal alcohol abuse and developmental problems (Down 1990). He described an area where the men worked as miners away from home. During their holiday they went home and were mostly drunk. So most children were conceived while their father was drunk. Developmental problems were quite common in that area.

Rudolf Steiner also described the effect of alcohol and stated that it matters if children are conceived under the influence of alcohol. The alcohol use of the father would influence the nervous system of the child and make it restless.

In medical literature not much research can be found in this area.

Bylander (1960) found that sons and daughters of alcoholic fathers had an increased risk of psychological problems, such as abdominal pains without a physical problem and depression. They achieved less in school, despite having the same intellectual capacity as the children from the central group.

Other researchers came to the same conclusion. It is of course likely that these problems are also related to growing up with an alcoholic father. How alcohol affects the semen has not been researched. One of our pupils has many of these problems. He has a moderate learning disability but it is his insecurity and behavioural problems which especially stand out. John came to us because of his enormous sense of failure coupled with weird, hyperactive and attention-seeking behaviour. He grew up with a drunken father and is slowly becoming conscious of his unusual background, no easy life for such a lad.

CHAPTER TEN

Prader-Willi Syndrome

It happens time and time again. A youngster with Prader-Willi Syndrome joins our boarding schools. Typically, the youngster is nice, friendly and outgoing, fits in well and seems to appreciate everything. But after a few months the stories change; the youngster can be quite anxious or difficult, steals food or is even aggressive on occasion. It needs some time for us to appreciate the deep-rooted social vulnerabilities such a youngster can have.

History

The first clear description of a person with Prader-(Labhart) Willi Syndrome is to be found in an essay by Langdon Down written in 1864 (Down 1990). He described a 21-year-old woman who had been mentally retarded from birth. She was 1.33 m tall and weighed 85 kg. Until the age of 7 she was of fine, thin build; after that she developed an enormous appetite. She had delicate hands and feet, hardly any secondary sexual characteristics at age 21, and no menstruation. She was short of breath and her weight presented quite a burden for her! Eventually she managed to lose weight under strict supervision on a diet of meat and water.

Doctors Prader and Willi recognized and described this syndrome in 1956 (O'Brien and Yule 1995). The estimated incidence of people with this syndrome is approximately 1 in every 15,000 live births; the syndrome can be found all over the world with boys and girls being equally affected. The adults are of short stature and often too heavy.

The male genitals are underdeveloped and the women have a late menarche or none at all. Feet and hands are small with fine bones. The face has a characteristic form with prominent forehead, narrow temples, almond shaped eyes and a mouth which appears triangular.

Brian

As a doctor I have been intensively involved with several young Prader-Willi Syndrome adults. One of these is Brian. He is the third child of healthy parents, his mother being a nurse and his father an engineer. Brian's mother recalls that she hardly experienced any foetal movements during pregnancy; the birth had to be induced and labour was long. Brian was floppy at birth, he produced a small cry and was put under observation in the special baby unit. He was so sleepy the first six weeks, he did not cry at all and feeding was a problem. For the first few days the mother tried to breast feed him but he couldn't suck and after that he had to be forced to drink out of a bottle for four months. He had to be woken to be fed during the night. He gained weight very slowly during his first year.

Brian's motor development was delayed and he started walking only at age 2. By age 5 he was dry and clean and out of nappies. He received speech therapy because of his unclear speech. Around age 3 his appetite suddenly changed and he could eat anything. He was fortunate in that the diagnosis Prader-Willi Syndrome was made early so his parents could keep him on a strict but healthy diet. Brian became used to the diet and no cupboards had to be locked.

Brian managed fairly well in school with some extra input. The educational psychologist made the parents appreciate that their child had very limited emotional ability. He learned to read but maths was more of a problem. He stayed somewhat socially isolated, probably due to the fact that he could be inflexible which could cause aggressive outbursts on occasion, even at home where his father was strong enough to cope.

Brian entered our school at age 17. We met a friendly, soft-spoken youngster with normal posture. The most striking feature was his anxious disposition. He did well in our surroundings and his independence could be increased; the supervision of his diet was more and more left to himself. However, slowly his weight started to increase and the rules had to be clarified.

Suddenly life became very tense and difficult leading to outbursts from Brian which required two male care workers to prevent him from harming other pupils. His lack of self-awareness prevented Brian from any insight as to his contribution to the outbursts and he would loudly complain about the received treatment, unfair in his opinion. The fact that he bruised very easily (like all Prader-Willi people) did not help as even holding his arm to prevent him from hitting out left blue marks.

It was difficult for Brian really to empathize with another person and not just perceive everything from his own perspective. This fact could make social interaction difficult as he tried, unconsciously, to form his world. We had to do something!

The decision was made to structure his life very clearly and to have firm consequences for unpleasant behaviour (loss of certain privileges). It was made clear that this was done out of respect to his person.

It was amazing to witness how Brian responded. The pleasant, interested and open person became visible again. The structure gave him a chance to show his real potential. Unfortunately we had to go through the same process a couple of times, each time reinforcing boundaries within which Brian could relax. When I approached his parents they made some general comments to complement the picture of Brian:

> He is not able to lead an independent life. He needs to be closely supervised to control eating. Brian can't entertain himself in that he doesn't read books, play games or watch television. He wants always to be organized and taken places. He has weak muscles and that means that he doesn't always get to the toilet in time.
>
> He still has no ability with numbers, so he can't handle money. You can't reason with him, if you try this will lead inevitably to tantrums. There is no depth to the conversation so the

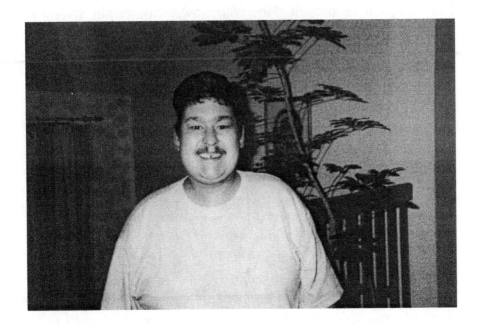

Hans, aged 22

conversation is limited, but he talks well when he meets people initially so this misleads people who only see him for a short time. They greatly overestimate his ability. He is very insecure, and needs a structured programme. What follows from this is that he doesn't respond well to sudden change in his routine. He is extremely immature, more like a 7-year-old than a 24-year-old. He has no interest in sex or girls. He is now on medication to control his tempers.

Hans

Hans' story shows a different side. On our first encounter it was immediately clear that he was special, with a weight of 110 kg and a height of 1.6 m. He walks slowly because of his weight. He has asthma and needs to use his inhaler. Otherwise he is an active chap with many hobbies and qualities. He is an excellent weaver, loves embroidery, and started a local chess club. He likes to talk a lot but fails to notice that his way of speaking can irritate others.

Life went well until Hans reached 21. He was the most capable trainee in a training centre for young adults, but also the most complicated. He needed a very clear and strong daily structure but the boundaries could become too narrow and he then talked about freedom and independence – a normal reaction for a young man of his age and intellectual development! He could not accept the given restrictions any more and became depressed.

In the end he had to be admitted to a local psychiatric ward for people with acute mental retardation and behavioural problems. Hans' weight on admission was 80 kg but soon rose to over 100 kg and he felt even more depressed.

All the professional staff slowly started to appreciate his real problems, see his loneliness and his social clumsiness. I attended a professional interdisciplinary meeting, with Hans present, and was shocked at the lack of insight regarding the consequences of his syndrome.

How different it was two months later. The speech therapist, who spoke while chewing a sweet, caused me to sit up a bit straighter. She tested Hans' speech and understanding and her conclusion was that he did not understand negatives! For example, the sentence 'The child does not run', he will understand as 'The child walks fast'. He would also need much more time really to comprehend connections; the lack of understanding could be the reason behind his aggressive response, 'Why?' when he is given a limitation.

As carers, what have we been saying? 'You are not allowed more than two slices of bread.' 'You are only allowed a piece of cake if you don't take any bread.' 'No, you cannot go alone to the shop.'

From then on we had to express everything in positive affirmations – 'You are allowed two slices of bread', 'Tomorrow you can go to the shop'. Our struggle with Hans was confirmed by our observations; all professional staff involved were in agreement and we began to have a glimpse of his inner life.

Meanwhile, Hans has found a new place to live where, through insight and experience, structure and freedom can be offered. As he expressed it: 'I am not seen as a syndrome there, but treated like a human being'. The future now holds more promise for Hans.

Description

These two life stories are very revealing. There are two phases visible in the life of a person with Prader-Willi Syndrome. The first phase lasts until the child is a toddler, the characteristics being summarized thus: there is hardly any movement during pregnancy, the new-born infant is floppy, has difficulties with feeding and therefore needs a lot of attention. Development is delayed. A drastic change will suddenly appear during the toddler stage: the floppy baby with feeding difficulties changes into a toddler with a ravenous appetite who can also develop temper tantrums. If a strict diet is not established and maintained, then a steady weight increase is to be expected.

These children are in general friendly, sleepy during the day, even to the point of drifting off to sleep. Lack of sleep has a negative effect on their moods.

With adults, life can be complicated by their obsessive behaviour, overeating and aggressive outbursts, both for the person and for their environment. Luckily, a diagnosis is now possible during the early years enabling parents to be prepared. In the case of Brian, the diet worked well as he had never been too heavy, but his behavioural problems could not be prevented. About 50 per cent of the Prader-Willi population will have some problems in this area, mostly aggressive outbursts which are often food related. Negativity, emotional imbalance, and picking and scratching their skin happen frequently. (Typically, should there be a midge bite or any other small spot, this will be scratched and picked to the extent that it can hardly heal.)

For some, doors will have to be locked, kitchen cupboards and larders are not always safe. Some people's appetite can be so extreme that even tasteless, inedible food will be eaten – whether it be cat food, dry milk powder, or the paper cover of a cake. Such stories are well known.

Despite every effort, these people will have a tendency to gain weight, even with a normal food intake. Their metabolic system needs fewer calories than the norm – 1000 calories a day is sufficient; for most of us this would mean a very restricted diet.

Richard Fried, an American doctor, gives the image of a human being who didn't outgrow certain aspects of the toddler phase. The soft stature is not well formed and there is a tendency to acquire a fatty deposit around the waist; the hair and skin can be lighter than would be expected within the family. The normal, friendly, outgoing behaviour can change into sudden attacks of tension and rage, reminding us of the phase which every 3 to 4-year old has to go through. Again, the egocentric attitude of a 3-year old is visible (Fried 1996).

The intellectual capacity can be compared with that of a 12-year-old: it is relatively well developed but stays concrete – abstract ideas remain incomprehensible. This discrepancy between intellectual and emotional development can create an enormous tension for people with Prader-Willi Syndrome and their environment.

Another way of understanding this syndrome is by looking at the contrast between the heavy, slow body, and the nervous eyes which register everything. These people know the daily routine of every carer. So they live with a clear polarity; the body is large, slow and sleepy, while their whole consciousness and awareness are concentrated in the periphery. The nimble fingers, the wakeful eyes and the picking of the skin seem to be an attempt to create a bodily awareness.

Similarly, the outbursts of temper can also be understood as expressing a need to penetrate their body. I noticed this particularly with a young man who could be very tense, but immediately after an outburst of temper he would be very 'present' within himself and it was possible to have quite a normal conversation with him. Unfortunately this did not last. Perhaps Hans meant the same when he said, 'I experience having Prader-Willi Syndrome as hovering above the earth'.

Sleepiness during the day is a symptom which indicates the dominance of the unconscious metabolic processes. If the weight continues to increase then a vegetative way of life starts to dominate and physical problems will pile up – high blood pressure, cardiovascular symptoms, breathing difficulties and diabetes mellitus are to be expected. Heart failure is the most common cause of death. It seems as if people with this syndrome can become sucked into a swamp and give up the struggle. Life expectancy is dependent on the control of the weight and could be normal with a normal weight.

People with Prader-Willi Syndrome do not have a well-developed social instinct – we might say that the heart forces do not stream. They are not readily aware of the intentions of others as their own emotional life is not sufficiently developed and they can be trapped in a life of diets, irritations and obsessions. This aspect of life needs attention but they will acknowledge this and be keen on artistic activities. Parents or members of staff should be conscious of their attitude to someone with the syndrome – a positive approach, with a lot of humour and care to avoid becoming irritated has been proved to work.

Psychological profile

It is clear that during the early years motor development and language are delayed. Problems with gross motor development, co-ordination and equilibrium persist into later life. Sometimes it can be difficult to understand children, not only due to the problem of articulation, but also due to the sound of their voice and their particular way of expressing themselves.

With regard to learning difficulties, there is in fact quite a range, varying from severe to very mild or borderline. However, the majority have moderate learning difficulties. Their visual skills are often excellent. They will spot everything! Reading skills are well developed and they have a wide vocabulary. Jigsaw puzzles are often a favourite. I know a few young people who are skilled weavers. However, their relationship to spoken information can be more of a problem; many have specific difficulties with maths, writing and short-term memory, and find it difficult to listen with concentration for a spell of time. Most people who work with them have a tendency to overestimate their abilities.

Neuroanatomy

Scientists have been trying for years to detect if the brains of people with Prader-Willi Syndrome are formed differently. The suggestion is that the hypothalamus is involved, and the dysfunction of the hypothalamus could explain the tendency to overeating, the short stature and the lack of sexual maturation. This hypothesis has never been confirmed; it appears that food intake is not dependent on certain aspects of the brain.

Sleep disturbances

Excessive sleepiness during the day, sleep apnoea (where breathing stops for short moments during sleep) and too superficial breathing during the day are characteristic of people with Prader-Willi Syndrome. The period during which they dream, so-called Rapid Eye Movement (REM) sleep, seems different. Most of us have regular periods of dream sleep, around 5 times a night. In people with Prader-Willi Syndrome, however, dream sleep is often interrupted, causing many short episodes of REM sleep.

After weight reduction, sleep apnoea will improve, but not the disturbances in REM sleep. Again, scientists conclude that the hypothalamus does not have optimal function as this organ is related to the regulation of sleeping and waking.

Approach

How do we help these people in daily life? The Prader-Willi Association is quite clear regarding the necessity of a clear structure with strict guidelines and understandable consequences. The co-ordinator for Britain formulates it as follows: 'I don't know a single person with Prader-Willi Syndrome in England [and she has met them all!] who can look after their own diet.'

I can fully agree with that out of my own experiences; a clear structure gives peace to the unformed emotional life. The real Brian became visible in this peace and could show his openness for religion.

How to do this is an enormous struggle for the carers. This is not too difficult with a 5-year-old child; it is still acceptable for a 15-year-old teenager who is developmentally delayed. But young adults want to experience their freedom. They will hardly accept limitations to this and can accuse their carers of treating them unfairly.

Prader-Willi Syndrome does not create the easiest of lives. Very often the syndrome comes to the foreground and can dominate the positive aspects of the personality. It requires an enormous effort to help create a reasonable lifestyle for these people.

It is heartening to meet people with this syndrome who have managed to give it a place in their lives. Inge, who has Prader-Willi Syndrome, learned to contain her own weight and focuses on collecting recipes. Still, she can feel cramped, and has become obsessed about any involvement with food. Fortunately she is able to recognize this and indicate how helpful the homoeopathic remedies are.

Paul, another young person I know, manages to control his weight with some support. He had been admitted to hospital at the age of 14 because he was overweight, but his weight is now healthy although it has to be controlled. He is well integrated into the therapeutic community; he may be more gentle in character than other youngsters of his age. His syndrome has withdrawn to the background and he appears as a young man with moderate learning difficulties.

Can we honestly know what is the inner experience, the fruit of a life full of unfulfilled longing? 'An angel is sitting next to my bed when I awake in the night,' says Inge.

Summary

During infancy:

- low muscle tone after birth
- feeding problems
- excessive sleep
- boys have underdeveloped genitalia
- delayed motor development.

Age 1 to 4 years:

- increased interest in food, which causes obesity
- temper tantrums.

Adults:

- low muscle tone
- obesity.

CHAPTER ELEVEN

Angelman Syndrome

Have you ever seen an angel in your life? The name 'Angelman Syndrome' is not derived from the fact that the children look so angelic but from the name of the doctor – Harry Angelman – who was the first person to describe this syndrome.

History

In 1965 Angelman had three learning-disabled children on his ward who had various problems but also many similarities. The children did not speak and had fixed smiles on their faces. They moved in a jerky way, had severe learning disabilities and suffered from epilepsy. He named this 'Happy Puppet Syndrome', a term that is no longer used but gives a lively description of the first impression these children can make (O'Brien and Yule 1995).

Description

Why should I describe this rare syndrome which affects only 1 in 20,000 children? In our schools we have 5 pupils with this condition, that is 5 per cent of our school population. This gives us ample opportunity to understand these children better, which is necessary as they are not easy or straightforward.

John, aged 13

John

John and I shared the same house for many years. He is a charming young man, as can be seen in the photo. He is fairly able compared to some of the other children with Angelman Syndrome, but otherwise his whole life story and behaviour are quite characteristic. I asked his mother to tell me more about his early years, and these are extracts from her letter:

> John was born, another little boy and brother for the older boy who was then 20 months old. Breast feeding didn't work, as he had difficulties latching on. John found it difficult to feed with the bottle. It took over an hour to feed him and he was mostly soon sick afterwards. Despite the sickness he was a beautiful baby who would smile between his bouts of sickness. He started

solids at 6 months. At 11 months I asked the GP to assess John. She was not concerned that he was not sitting alone, was still constantly sick and was not drinking. At 15 months I asked for another assessment, he was only putting on ½ ounce a week. The paediatrician said that some babies made themselves sick for attention...

John was seen at 17 months by another paediatrician who said that John's development was delayed – I was devastated. He suggested physiotherapy to help John to walk alone and a teacher for manipulative, cognitive skills. Investigations were done, all normal. At 22 months he got medication for the emptying of his stomach, I felt I was a neurotic mother. I was desperate for help as the medicine made no difference. I took a plastic bag full of sick-wet bibs that John had gone through the morning of his appointment and asked if this was normal. Only then were we referred to a surgeon.

He received, after many cancellations because of a cold, a fundoplication [stomach operation to prevent food coming back up into the gullet] at last at age 2½ and his sickness stopped. We were in hospital for five days and I wished that I could have the operation as he couldn't understand the various procedures.

John's squint was corrected at 2 years 2 months. This involved a two-night stay at another hospital and numerous visits to the ortoptist [a specialist in eye movements]. When John was 3½ it was decided that he had left and right divergence on occasion, especially when tired, but could use both eyes.

In the meantime John had regular physiotherapy involving splints to help pelvic control and boots to help his ankles. He walked alone just before his fundoplication.

We had one visit from a preschool, peripatetic teacher who said we were doing the right things and that however things turned out, John would always be our John – a very loving, lovable little boy who seemed very happy.

We began potty training, never dreaming that John would be 14 years old before we stopped needing nappies at night.

John began day-care nursery one day a week. He was very upset and cried constantly until Week Five when he cried for five minutes then played, sat at the table for lunch, fed himself with his hands, sat for the story and pointed to his shoes.

Portage began – a clinical psychologist visited us at home once a week – setting small targets e.g. John had to hold his spoon every mealtime.

When John was 3 years old, the paediatrician began the statementing process involving medical and psychological assessments. He had his first chromosome test which was pronounced normal.

At 3 years 5 months John began full-time nursery at a school for children with severe learning difficulties. He was transported by minibus. Edna was his bus lady. A retired grandma who had and still has a soft spot for our delicate little smiley John, she was to hold his hand all the way to school and back.

John was a very active little boy who needed constant supervision to keep him from harm. He had a fascination with plastic bags and would snatch and empty one as if his life depended on it and then feel it and fold it up and eventually put it into his mouth. This habit continued until fairly recently as he can now control his urge better.

We had to bolt John's bed to the floor and tie the mattress to the base so he couldn't dismantle it and pull the carpet up underneath it. John took his curtains down, his curtain rail, blind, lampshade, pictures, mobiles. We had to put wooden shutters on his window and a lock on his door so he couldn't get out during the night and hurt himself. Even now his bedroom is quite bare to stop him fiddling with things as this prevents him from sleeping. [He has a normal room with curtains.]

John's older brother Will was very tolerant of John pulling his hair, biting him and destroying his pictures, toys or models. We had stopped friends visiting as we didn't want their children bitten or smacked. We were unable to chat as John determined all my attention and going out was often a nightmare. John had screamed in a pushchair which faced people so we had bought another one which faced me, but now he would grab people or their bags. If we went out to eat he would throw or knock things over and laugh.

We tried 'friends and family' – a scheme whereby a couple take your special child for a few hours a week once they have got to know him (which took a good few months). In practice it didn't work out as they would cancel at the last minute when John was ready to go and it was so erratic that it was not helpful. Crossroads care proved more useful, and John still goes out once a week in his holidays on the bus to a town or park with the carer he knows well.

John had two years at the special schools, but he didn't seem to be making any progress and his behaviour was increasingly disruptive and challenging.

On day I was chatting to my former boss and she happened to mention Botton Village and Camphill. I had a vague recollection of my mum telling me about a lady at church who was having a coffee morning to raise funds for the Camphill school that her son attended as a sort of boarder. I said that she must be a heartless woman to send her son away and how could anyone do such a thing. But the seed was sown. I found Botton and eventually the Camphill Rudolf Steiner Schools and got each prospectus. The Aberdeen School stood out for me as the place where the Camphill movement had begun and after many tears and heart searching we went for an informal visit. As soon as we entered the Camphill Estate I knew this was the right place for John to learn, to develop to achieve his potential. I couldn't answer the doctor's questions [during the interview] I was in such an emotional turmoil. John pulled the glasses and the scarf from the lady showing us around. I didn't think we would be offered a place. But after many interviews, letters, assessments, phone calls John started at Camphill when he was 7 ½ years old. It was the best and hardest decision we ever had to make.

John had an operation to lengthen his Achilles tendons, which were so short he could only walk on tiptoes, when he was 9½ years old. His lower legs were in plaster for weeks and he had to go back to his big pushchair again. He needed more physiotherapy and continues to wear supportive boots to keep his heels down.

At 7½ years John had another chromosome test and that too proved normal. At almost 13 years old John had another chromosome test and saw a geneticist who thought that there was a good possibility that John had Angelman Syndrome. This was confirmed when John was 16 years old. I wish we could have had an earlier diagnosis, which would have helped us to understand John's behaviour and medical problems more.

John will be 17 next week. It is difficult to see him as a young man and not a little boy who still loves cuddles. He is able to say about a dozen words, not always clearly, and normally makes himself understood to people who know him. He smiles as he walks along and laughs, often uncontrollably, if something amuses him.

He is generally much calmer and he will help with household tasks willingly. He is trying hard to control the laughter, which can be inappropriate. He needs the security of people who know him or his behaviour can be unpredictable. He understands more than he can express and he is empathetic.

He enjoys doing jigsaw puzzles (up to about 100 pieces) and he can now sit and concentrate alone quite happily. We are still struggling with chronic constipation after various investigations. John has daily laxatives. He now eats and drinks well. He enjoys his active school life, which addresses every aspect of his development in a calm, supportive, nurturing atmosphere. He also enjoys his holidays at home: horse-riding, going in the car or on the bus, hanging out with Will.

John has many typical symptoms of Angelman Syndrome and we have had a bumpy journey so far. The ride is not over yet, but what a lovely companion we have.

This letter from John's mother highlights many issues which are common for children with special needs and their family. Parents have to bear the medical appointments, doctors who say it will be all right, being labelled as neurotic, the long road to find help, social withdrawal from friends and the mixed feelings about having to send the child to a residential school. They have to find in themselves never-ending love and commitment.

It took a long time before the geneticist diagnosed John. But I was alerted, after observing him closely, to the possibility of Angelman Syndrome because of his laughter and his behaviour, which reminded me of the other children with Angelman Syndrome.

How do we recognize a child with this syndrome?

Infancy

The pregnancy is usually normal, and nothing seems unusual at birth. Problems with sucking and swallowing can arise and some babies bring up their food. They are sociable and laugh a lot between 3 and 6 months, with their tongues sometimes hanging out of their mouths. At age 6 to 12 months, the slower motor development becomes obvious and it seems that these children develop spasms.

Age 1 to 3 years

The problems become more visible and often the diagnosis is made in these years. The head can be small; epileptic seizures may start although they are not always apparent. The EEG shows specific disturbances. These are not related to the epilepsy or to the episodic periods of laughter, and are also visible during sleep. This EEG pattern can be helpful in making the diagnosis with young children. It is during this period that behaviour can become more problematic. The children are often hyperactive and they seem to be in constant movement. This, combined with the protruding tongue and dribbling, gives them a characteristic appearance. They are prone to bouts of laughter, especially when excited. No speech development is apparent.

Age 3 to 8 years

Children with Angelman Syndrome often learn to walk during this period. This can be difficult due to low muscle tension and the fact that their movements are jerky. The epilepsy can be difficult to control although the fits themselves are not severe. Most children become toilet trained. Simple things like eating and dressing can be difficult because of the movement disturbances. Sleep can be very problematic. The children often require a specially adjusted room to guarantee their safety and to prevent the curtains being pulled down.

Age 8 onwards

The children continue to develop slowly but surely. They can learn simple tasks such as setting the table, pushing a wheelbarrow, etc. Speech never develops. They enjoy good health in general and have a normal life expectancy. The epilepsy can decrease and at age 16 can sometimes disappear. The EEG becomes normal yet the typical laugh remains. When watching pupils of our school at play, I often hear some of them burst into fits of laughter at exciting moments – these are the children with Angelman Syndrome. The laughter can be a response to any emotion, be it happiness, tension or fear. These children are very open and outgoing. They like to make eye contact, they gaze at you with their light blue eyes and you find yourself falling into an unknown depth as you meet no resistance, no sign of antipathy in their gaze. Full of enthusiasm, they approach any visitor, shake his hand and kiss him until the shocked visitor realizes that the kiss has transformed into a bite, and the hand has suddenly started to scratch. Sometimes my patience was stretched to breaking point if a child with Angelman Syndrome pulled the hair of an innocent child with a radiant smile on his face. However, it is useless to become cross as strong words just call forth more laughter.

Language

One of the most striking features of many of these children is their inability to speak. As babies they don't start to babble and few are able to say more than a few words through childhood. Research has shown that their physical ability to speak is disturbed; they are not aware of how to use the muscles of their mouth and the ability to use sign language is also limited. Still, the ability to understand and grasp language clearly surpasses the ability to use it. A few of the youngsters will use their own signs or symbols to communicate. The memory of these children is often excellent, especially regarding human faces and spatial orientation.

The innate openness of these children can pose a problem for new carers. Take, for example, Maurice – 17 years old with lanky and gangly limbs, a small head, an open face and a wide grin. For ten years he has been a boarder in our school, but that did not prevent him from regressing when a new carer started to work with him. He screamed more, wet himself, couldn't stop laughing, could no longer do his chores and threw objects across the room. When the carer got cross and raised his voice, this had the opposite effect to the one desired, and Maurice became more restless. However, the carer was a very perceptive young man and quickly learned his lesson. He had to master a certain inner attitude, and this holds true for every new carer who works with a child with Angelman Syndrome. Angelman children require a specific approach. They are very open, outgoing, friendly and laughing. If you go along with this too much they will lose themselves and become too excited. It is amazing to see how their behaviour improves when they are approached without too much emotion or expectation. Carers have to be careful to hold themselves back, maybe even to avoid eye contact, because the eye contact can be too strong a trigger for the children and cause them to become excited.

Neurology

I looked earlier at the neuroanatomy of the people with this syndrome. In the brain are specialized areas for certain abilities, e.g. speech and reasoning; but the brain works essentially as a whole and other parts of the brain can compensate for a problem in one area. There is not much information or research into the neuroanatomy of the brain. The brains of people with Angelman Syndrome are smaller than normal, which is clear in that their head circumference is also often smaller than average. Some neurological abnormalities have been found, such as cerebellar hyperplasia (cerebellum is overdeveloped) and unilateral temporal hyperplasia (overdeveloped temporal lobe on one side) – the temporal lobe is associated with speech and language, so maybe this can give some explanation. Further differences included decreased myelinization (formation of myelin sheaths around nerve cells) and thinning of the corpus callosum. The corpus callosum provides the link between the left and right brain.

Children with Angelman Syndrome often have a characteristic way of walking with very widespread arms and legs, as if the right and left sides of the body do not meet in the middle. Epilepsy occurs in 90 per cent of children with Angelman Syndrome, so a certain excitability of the cortex is also typical.

Life processes

Studying the neuroanatomical structures can help towards our understanding of the child with this condition, but I also want to introduce an additional way of enabling this understanding to come about. In children with this condition, there seems to be a lot of unconscious activity which expresses itself in their hyperactivity, laughter and epilepsy.

Life processes and soul life

Within our human system are life processes which make it possible to live. These are breathing, warming, metabolism, secretion (sweat, faeces, urine etc.), maintenance, growth, maturation and reproduction. These processes are the foundation of normal life and work better when they remain unconscious. As soon as we become conscious of these bodily activities we feel disturbed: for example, shortness of breath creates fear. We need to feel a degree of warmth but a fever knocks us out and puts us in bed; cold can also hinder us – we can't fall asleep with icy feet. Metabolic processes are not conscious and take place in the glands and organs. While secretion is easily observed in the production of saliva, urine and transpiration, the secretion of digestive juices is usually not observed.

We can summarize the life processes as follows: we encounter the world in a rhythmical fashion through breathing; we then warm the air and make it our own, thereby humanizing everything we encounter. Through metabolic processes, we take in substances from the world. Secretion is a turning point – we begin to break down substances and make them our own. Maintenance requires constant renewal of the substances of our body. Growth and development are the final result and lead to the highest goals in life – maturation as an individual or the creation of a new human being through reproduction.

The reason why I discuss this at some length here is that these life processes can be especially helpful in understanding children with special needs. The study of these processes is an important tool in 'curative education'. They are not the same as physiological processes such as the exchange of oxygen in the lungs. As I perhaps indicated in my description, these processes also have a place in our soul experience of the world. For instance, as we breathe in air we also breathe in life experiences (perception). We then have to learn from our experiences – become enthusiastic about them (warmth), so that we can make them our own (concept), then let the experiences change (metabolize) into understanding so that we can feel enriched by them (memory). This describes the first three processes, but how is it with the other processes, which relate to our 'will' – the unconscious ability to act? In order to clarify the soul quality of these processes let us examine different aspects of our will.

'Instinct' is the most basic form of will and relates to the process of secretion. In the animal kingdom we can marvel as we observe the quality of instinct as it relates to secretion: bees, wasps, spiders and even some bird species secrete their own building material. We all know of the rich-smelling honeycomb, craftily secreted and formed by the bees. In humans this process is more hidden. One small example is the saliva that runs in our mouth as we think about, or smell, food.

The next will process is 'drive'. Drive is visible in the animal world in the maintenance of the species; the drive to find food and create a shelter is also visible in us.

The next process, 'desire', is less of a necessity and allows more freedom than 'instinct' and 'drive'. Desire allows us to be interested, to long for, people, activities, training, a new house. It facilitates inner development.

The highest quality of our will is 'motivation'. Here we are really free: we make choices without necessity. I am motivated to spend this Sunday morning at my writing desk. Through motivation we allow individuality to shine. Nelson Mandela is still the most outstanding example for me: his motivation and choices led to 23 years of imprisonment; released from prison he emerged as a free person, not embittered by his experiences, ready and able to guide his country as the first black president of South Africa.

To summarize:

Life process	Related soul process
Breathing	Perception
Warming	Concept
Metabolism	Memory
Secretion	Instinct
Maintenance	Drive
Growth	Desire
Maturation and reproduction	Motivation

So how do these concepts help us better to understand children with Angelman Syndrome? As I mentioned before, these life processes are normally unconscious. We can observe how the newborn baby is still totally submerged, dependent on these processes. The infant is hungry, so he cries, he drinks his fill of contentment at his mother's breast as his little feet move along with it. The life processes dominate the life of the baby. Slowly these processes become unconscious.

The child with Angelman Syndrome and life processes

This process is different in children with Angelman Syndrome, where the life processes maintain their active presence and are too dominant. These children will have difficulty with the rhythmical 'in and out' breathing of the world. They 'exhale' too much; they are too open to sense impressions. The process of 'naming' these sense impressions, of transforming the perceptions into concepts, is also disturbed. The sensory world remains fragmented and unconceptualized. The next process of memory, of active working memory, is also limited. Their will is often not very free, but is bound to instinctive activities or related to 'drive'. Slowly, with a lot of effort, we manage to help the children to grow, to mature and to develop their inner space. Every experience calls forth an immediate reaction. The sense perception bounces back, and the child starts to laugh, the limb moves and the hand can suddenly scratch. It is important to realize that the negative behaviour is not naughtiness but a reflex: the child stays in the world of sense perceptions and finds it difficult really to internalize or 'digest' experiences.

Treatment

Progress will be slow but it will happen – that is the encouraging fact for these children. They are disastrous sleepers, they can pull down the curtains and pictures, but things will improve. In general, they slow down, relax over time and can learn simple skills. Every child is unique and different, and so are these special children. Young children will need an individualized programme based on their specific needs. The children in our school are a little older, between 7 and 18, and benefit from a full programme of activities. From a special therapeutic point of view they all receive massage with special etheric oils to help relaxation. For children and teenagers, exercises to stimulate balance, sensory integration and movement are important. Learning to balance on a bench, throwing balls and going for walks in wooded areas will all help the child to feel more confident when moving. Physiotherapy can also be required, and horse-riding therapy has been used quite successfully. While riding, the child has to focus on the animal and often the grimace on the face disappears and the child can focus. Horse-riding is helpful for the following reasons: the children have a particular abnormality in their gait, which means that the movement of the pelvic region, vital to a wide range of bodily functions, is not properly executed. The horse, when moving in the 4x4 rhythm of the walk, produces those complex movements and rhythms in the area of the saddle which are produced in a normal walk. These movements can be passed on from the horse to the rider very strongly and directly, especially when riding bare-back. Thus the rider can receive direct physiotherapy from the horse.

Angelman children do not often show sufficient ability to differentiate between the living world and the world of objects. Coming into contact with horses can help them to appreciate an animate being. Well-trained horses can learn to tolerate the rough, and at times even aggressive, behaviour of the Angelman child.

Epilepsy can be a problem for many children and appropriate treatment is required here. This will require involvement from the child's doctor. Complementary medicines based on anthroposophy may be used to support this process, to help the children to become sturdier and more relaxed in themselves.

Hyperactivity

The most obvious symptom of these children is their hyperactivity – they are constantly in motion and have a short concentration span. Babies and toddlers seem endlessly active – they always have a toy in their hands or mouths. The constant movement can be so pronounced that the child has difficulties with social interaction and does not have the peace to perceive facial expressions. This behaviour makes the children appear more disabled than they really are. As mentioned before, this improves with age and children can do relatively well.

Balance

Another aspect of Angelman Syndrome is the poor sense of balance – physical as well as 'soul' balance – in children with this condition.

They move through the world as if it is flat, not seeming to be aware of depth or of the space behind them. (This could be related to the underdevelopment of the corpus callosum which connects the right and left hemispheres of the brain.) Some children become more aware of their limitations in puberty and feel even more insecure, which can lead to further deterioration in movement and balance. This poor sense of orientation can cause anxiety. With Maurice, whom I mentioned earlier, we observed how a physical exercise programme enhanced his inner balance: he visited the gym a few times a week to do balance exercises and slowly grew in confidence. Courage is very important, especially for the movement of the disturbed child. It can require enormous courage just to step over a tree trunk if you have a degree of ataxia. Behind the open, radiant faces a lot of anxiety is hidden; every activity, every step of development, helps the child to feel more secure.

Summary

In 100 per cent of diagnosed cases

- developmental delay (functionally severe)
- speech impairment: no speech or minimal use of words; receptive and non-verbal communication skills are higher than verbal ones
- movement or balance disorder: usually ataxia of gait and/or tremulous movement of limbs
- behavioural uniqueness: any combination of the following – frequent laughing/smiling; apparent happy demeanour; easily excitable personality, often with hand flapping movements; hyperactive behaviour; short attention span.

Frequent occurrence (more than 80 per cent of diagnosed cases)

- delayed, disproportionate growth in head circumference
- abnormal EEG (characteristic pattern).

Associated (20 per cent–80 per cent of diagnosed cases)

- flat occiput, occipital groove
- protruding tongue, protruding upper jaw, wide mouth
- frequent drooling, excessive chewing/mouthing behaviours
- hypopigmented (too little pigment) skin, hair and eyes (only in deletion cases)
- hyperactivity in lower extremity and deep tendon reflexes
- uplifted, flexed arm position, especially during ambulation
- sleep disturbance
- attraction to/fascination with water.

(From Williams, Angelman, *et al.* 1995, p.238)

CHAPTER TWELVE

Angelman and Prader-Willi Syndromes
A Polarity

These two syndromes are mentioned in almost every book on genes. Why is this? Do the writers of these books have a special interest in people with these syndromes? On the contrary, I suspect that many of these writers have never even met a person with one of these conditions. This was poignantly illustrated when I spoke to a local 'expert' on the diagnosis of these conditions via the genes. This lady travels worldwide to conferences on the diagnosis of Prader-Willi and Angelman syndromes, but knows these conditions only from a genetic point of view: she has never encountered anyone with either syndrome.

So why are scientists so fascinated with these conditions? It is because, despite the differences between the two conditions, Angelman and Prader-Willi Syndromes are related to the same chromosome and even an identical part of this chromosome: in both, a part of the long arm of Chromosome 15 is missing, specifically the markers q11 to q13. The difference is in the origin of the chromosomal deletion: a person with Angelman inherits it from the maternal Chromosome 15 while a person with Prader-Willi inherits from the paternal. The latest research shows that the genes involved are not exactly the same length, although they are at the same location. This phenomenon is called 'genomic printing': this means that genetic material is expressed differently if it comes from the father rather than the mother.

Genetic background

So what will a geneticist look for? If the doctors involved in a diagnosis suspect one of these two syndromes but are uncertain which of them it may be, then a blood sample will be taken. In the laboratory, it will be checked to see if the relevant section of Chromosome 15 has been inherited from both the father and the mother, so-called 'bi-parental inheritance'. If this is the case you can be 100 per cent sure that the person does not have Prader-Willi Syndrome, because in this condition either the inherited part from the father is missing, or there will be two alleles (genetic members) from the mother. Bi-parental inheritance also excludes Angelman Syndrome in 70–80 per cent of cases. Often a person with Angelman Syndrome will have two paternal alleles, but he or she can have bi-parental inheritance of those specific alleles.

In 20–30 per cent of the cases, a mutation or microdeletion happens in the same markers on Chromosome 15, q11 to q13. It was found that Prader-Willi Syndrome relates to four genes while in Angelman Syndrome just one gene is affected. The children with Angelman Syndrome who miss their maternal allele of Chromosome 15 are the children with the more classical symptoms – fair haired, blue eyed, with poor balance and quite limited in their abilities. The other children – those who have a mutation – can have dark hair and be less disabled. Of course, no two persons with a syndrome are the same and we should be careful not to have preconceived ideas.

This was especially clear to me when I visited a study day for families with children with Angelman Syndrome. I was quite amazed when I entered the room and looked around: had I misunderstood and come to a different meeting? There were two boys: one was a big, well-built boy who moved without jerking and could walk quite normally. Both were able to communicate actively with signs. They might have had Prader-Willi Syndrome, except that they couldn't speak and clearly had a severe intellectual disability and other signs of

Angelman Syndrome. 'Great guy,' said the father, radiant when he mentions his son.

Polarity

While I was considering these two different ways of being, it came to me that it must be quite different to live the life of a person with Angelman Syndrome or Prader-Willi Syndrome. You would have quite opposite experiences of life. Table 12.1 shows my attempt to think this through.

Table 12.1 Polarity between Angelman and Prader-Willi Syndromes		
Characteristic	Angelman Syndrome	Prader-Willi Syndrome
Missing part	Maternal Chromosome 15 q11 to q13	Paternal Chromosome 15 q11 to q13
Physical appearance	Thin (as a child)	Round, overweight
Muscle tone	Too high (spastic)	Too low (hypotonic)
Appetite	Poor eaters	Can't stop eating
Epilepsy	Usually	Not normally
Sleep	Problematic, especially for children	Sleeps a lot, can fall asleep in the daytime
Speech	No speech and limited sign language	Likes to speak (can't stop sometimes)
Development level	Quite intellectually disabled	Reasonable intelligence
Soul attitude	Open, no antipathy	Ego-centric
Behaviour	Overstimulated but passive	Friendly; can have outbursts of temper
Relationship to the world	Passive, reacts, waits till the world comes	Keen interest in the surroundings (wants to know everything)

This could lead one to wonder about the different qualities of the maternal and paternal hereditary streams. The twenty-first century sees a less strict division between 'male' and 'female' qualities, but it is true to say that women have a soft, rounder body form in general and men are more muscular. Somebody once observed that women are 'soft on the outside but tough on the inside': women live longer, are relatively tough and often seem to cope better with pain. During the time that I sutured wounds as a GP, I was amazed at how big guys would faint at the sight of their own blood, so perhaps we could tentatively say that 'men are hard on the outside and soft on the inside'. This is, of course, a gross oversimplification but I will leave it there to continue my line of thought: in Angelman Syndrome we observe, especially during childhood, a more thin, hardened body and a passive, very open soul attitude which lets the world in. So there is a body with more male qualities combined with a soul constitution which is traditionally seen as female. When you observe people with Prader-Willi Syndrome you see a more soft, unformed body with an outgoing, active soul life. We could tentatively say – a more female body with a more male-oriented soul attitude. To summarize:

Angelman Syndrome	Prader-Willi Syndrome
Lacks maternal part of Chromosome 15	Lacks paternal part of Chromosome 15
Physical body has a more 'male' quality	Physical body has a more 'female' quality
Soul attitude has a more 'female' tendency	Soul attitude has a more 'male' tendency

With this polarity, it is quite clear that we have left pure scientific thinking behind us and tried to enter the world of images and archetypes. This is one example and I hope it will stimulate the reader to create other images.

'Genes are not there to cause disease,' writes Matt Ridley in his fascinating book *Genome* (1999; p.207). They are not, but we have observed how small changes in our genetic material can colour someone's biography. I still find it quite strange that missing such a small part of Chromosome 15 can have these far-reaching consequences. On the other hand, I know people with one or even two X chromosomes too many, and they live quite normally. Men with Klinefelter

Syndrome (XXY), for example, wouldn't stand out in normal life. I know a young woman with four X chromosomes who is managing her life with support, and women with Turner Syndrome (who have 45 chromosomes, missing one X) can also have a normal life.

Expression

It is also good to realize that there is not always a linear relationship between a genetic configuration and its appearance. The term 'expression' covers this. *Smith's Recognisable Patterns of Human Malformations* (K.L. Jones 1997) says that 'expression is the degree of abnormality' caused by a genetic variation – the expression can be normal, mild or even absent. Persons with a genetic variation can show different degrees of expression. In other words, there is no linear relationship between genetic abnormalities and their expression: the individuality of a person and his or her environment both play a role, creating space for variation. Despite the same genetic abnormality, there are differences in expression.

CHAPTER THIRTEEN

Wolf-Hirschhorn Syndrome

This is a rare syndrome, and it poses some radical questions about quality of life. Children with this syndrome are missing a part of Chromosome 4, which has far-reaching consequences. They have prenatal growth retardation and are born with a low birth weight. Many abnormalities are visible at birth, after which their growth retardation continues. The small head has a typical form, the ears are low set and large, the eyebrows have a high arch, the nose is beaked with a broad base and the jaw is small. The muscle tone of the children is low and they often have skeletal abnormalities, severe scoliosis (curvature of the spine) being the most common. Epilepsy is quite common and can be difficult to control. These children can have problems with hearing and vision, 50 per cent have congenital heart defects and frequent chest infections are also common. Kidney abnormalities are also part of the picture. Their intellectual development is quite limited; the children never learn to speak and are also restricted in other forms of communication. Their life expectancy is short; many children die young, some as adolescents, while others can reach the age of 30.

Ronald

Ronald had this rare syndrome. It is not easy to forget him once you have met him. He was 18 years old but still very small, not even 1.25m tall, and he appeared smaller because of his crooked back. Ronald was rather quiet, would hardly ever make any sounds, nor would he scream or laugh. He would not look you in the eye, turning

Ronald

his eyes upwards. Ronald needed an enormous amount of support. As a baby he was very vulnerable and could sleep and sleep. His mother sensed that he would just die in his sleep if she didn't wake him up – he seemed to lack the energy to wake himself. He learned to walk when he was 5 years old and slowly he became stronger. By the age of 18 he could move his hands, clap, stroke his mother's hair and feed himself with a spoon.

Epileptic fits bothered him a few times a week, after which he needed to sleep. When he was 16, he had a particularly heavy attack and we feared for his life. Ronald required constant care. His communication was very subtle and his carer needed to be really in tune with his needs. His health was quite poor and he needed a lot of sleep. When ill he slept for most of the day. During the last two years, his general well-being had declined; his walking was more difficult and his balance had deteriorated. Both were probably caused by the increasing scoliosis of his back.

Ronald appeared, to the superficial observer, as a passive person but he had quite an important place in his house community and in his class. The other children appreciated his presence and liked to draw him into activities. His mother had a very close connection to him and hoped he could move back to the west coast near her home, where they were building a specially designed small house for him and other youngsters with special needs. This would enable her to visit him more frequently, as our school is on the east coast of Scotland – a five-hour journey away.

Ronald always smiled when he saw his mother, but it is wrong to assume that Ronald gained this inner tranquillity just like that. We could observe a clear development. He arrived in our school when he was 11 years old and was emotionally still very young in himself. He was quite isolated during his first year in our school because of his spitting, and his noisy behaviour could disturb the class – he would tap his feet on the ground or flap with his hands and be totally engrossed in this. Slowly he became part of the group and could partake in the atmosphere of the class. His eye contact increased, he was not so easily upset, and the periods when he was very tense and bit his hands reduced.

As mentioned before, by the age of 18 his physical strength had lessened, but the amazing thing to observe was that he appeared more emotionally balanced and had gained more inner peace. In the Camphill schools all children follow the full curriculum – they learn about Greek history, history of art, biology and physics independent of their intellectual ability. This is the first part of the school morning. In the second part of the morning, they will have a tailor-made programme to address their specific disability. Ronald had to change in order to be part of all this teaching and we saw that this approach helped him to feel part of his peer group, to feel part of the development of people of his age.

It is a yearly custom at Camphill that everybody climbs a Scottish hill on Ascension Day, and of course Ronald came along. He sat on the shoulders of a carer or some of the older, stronger pupils helped to carry him. Ronald's presence was especially important for John, a young man with a mild learning disability who got into trouble at home and came to our school. John could relax in Ronald's presence — a carer once described it like this: 'Ronald is the opposite of a modern cool teenager; he is not beautiful, his back is not straight, he has spots and he is surely not sexy, but he is a personality'.

I wrote to his mother for an update on Ronald's life a couple of years later. Ronald had moved back by then to the west coast. This is what she wrote back:

> Ronald has settled really well in 'An Granian' and enjoys the company of the other four residents. He has changed quite a lot since his return to Oban. He is much more mature and has developed a wicked sense of humour. Now that the staff know him better, they are able to understand his needs and feelings. He still has that serene and calming effect on others, and staff often ask to work with him if they are feeling a bit stressed or down, as he is usually happy to give them a smile and a hug. His health has been good most of the time, although he still gets the occasional cold or sore throat. During the first year he was back in Oban, Ronald's seizures were quite frequent and very worrying, so the consultant at the hospital gradually changed his medication and now his seizures are better controlled. They are not occurring as often, and usually [are] not too severe, unless he is unwell in himself. He has been stronger, and happy and his walking is good most days, unless he is tired or unwell.
>
> It is good to have Ronald back in Oban, only a ten-minute drive from my house. I see him every day and am very involved in his day-to-day life. His brother studies but comes back every second or third weekend to spend some time with Ronald, and they are still very close.

We cannot value Ronald's life by observing what he has achieved successfully in his life; his deeds are not visible. However, if we widen our gaze and observe what happens in the space around him, we perceive a different image. We see that he calls forth qualities in other people they didn't otherwise show and creates human encounters between the people who stand around him. Ronald is active in an unconscious way in his surroundings. An image arises of a human being passing his life in a meditative quality – uncomplaining and peaceful. He has periods of restlessness and tension but, if he feels recognized and cared for in the right way, he relaxes.

We can also understand the value of his life from a totally different point of view. As mentioned before, the basic philosophy of Camphill is that every human being, independent of race, sex or handicap, has a healthy inner personality. Rudolf Steiner inaugurated a Christian philosophy with reincarnation at its centre. According to anthroposophy, every human being develops during repeated earth lives. Steiner has spoken about the lives of certain famous personalities and pointed out that quite often those famous personalities experienced a 'rest' incarnation in a former incarnation – a life as a person with developmental problems. What does this mean? Should we accept this as true, or is it just a statement that we can take or leave? Rudolf Steiner always puts great emphasis on the fact that anthroposophy is not a 'belief system' but has to be tested by our own experiences and thoughts. So I always struggle with this far-reaching statement and I realize that it can appear strange for the reader. I was quite struck when I read a similar thought in a totally different context. Rabbi Yonassan Gershom is a Jewish rabbi who wrote about the destiny of the Jewish people in the Second World War. He says:

> Consider, for example, a soul who has spent many lives as a learned scholar. Between incarnations, the soul decides that it has mastered the intellectual plane and now wants to learn more about relating to people through the heart. In order to accomplish this as quickly as possible, it might choose a body that is mentally retarded. Without the ability to use the intellect, the soul will have no choice but to learn to communicate through feelings and emotions. If all goes well, the soul will be born into a loving, heart-filled environment where it will be nurtured and cared for as a fellow human being. After a full, rich life as a retarded citizen, the soul will return to the spiritual world,

having succeeded in what it wanted to learn. (Gershom 1992, pp.162–163)

Seen from this perspective, Ronald's life takes on a different meaning and we could pose the question: are we not encountering here an individual who is further developed than we are? Seen from this point of view we can understand the feelings of reverence and selflessness he calls forth in his environment. Living with this question, it seems to me that many children with a learning disability have taken on this destiny out of a conscious decision, maybe even out of a sacrifice. I experience it especially with severely disabled children who are suffering from a degenerative illness and have a short life expectancy.

While I was writing this chapter, somebody made a remark to me regarding Kwan, a small Indian boy with a rare metabolic illness. He has the body of a toddler, although he is 9 years old, and lives in his own world. Occasionally, clear-sounding laughter can be heard. His body is slowly stiffening and his life expectancy is limited. Already, his walking has deteriorated. He is a beautiful child who gives us concern when he stops eating or laughing. Everybody loves him and because of his peaceful radiance he is the centre of the house community. The remark was: 'When I work with Kwan I experience a giant.' Who knows the ways of destiny?

CHAPTER FOURTEEN

The Sun Cross

One of my favourite activities is to hunt for new books in a bookshop, and that is how I happened to come across the book *In the Blood* by Steve Jones (1997), the famous London professor of genetics. The title of his last chapter, 'Death or Resurrection', struck me. It was the same title that I had in mind for this concluding chapter. In his last chapter, there is a reproduction of a painting by Grünewald – 'The Resurrection of Christ'. This painting has a special meaning for me. It is part of the so-called 'Isenheimer Altar' and can still be admired in Colmar, France. The Isenheimer Altar is a triptych, i.e. an altarpiece in which three scenes are depicted: the Resurrection of Christ, the Visitation of the holy Antonius and the Crucifixion of Christ. Grünewald attempted to create a piece of 'healing art' – the sick would visit the chapel and form an inner connection to the scenes on the altarpiece. Grünewald's 'Resurrection' is magnificent and reassuring. The Crucifixion of Christ and the Visitation of Antonius are very real and frightening.

Returning to the book by Professor Jones, the question he poses is – is there truly a resurrection, or are we all doomed to death? Steve Jones approached this question from a genetic perspective and his conclusion is that when individuals die they will live on in their genes. According to him, our resurrection can be found in sexual activity and procreation. Jones' point of view is made very convincingly, with colourful descriptions, but where does it leave human beings with genetically determined developmental problems? They will mostly remain childless. Are they then victims of Darwin's law of the survival of the fittest?

Darwin was a very sharp observer. His autobiography is fascinating to read (Darwin 1958). As a young man, he was more interested in sport, leisure and shooting than in study. The most important event in his life was a five-year long journey on board a ship called the *Beagle*. He was part of a journey of discovery, and he went along as a naturalist. He boarded as a religious person, but what he saw on the journey convinced him that no God could have created the world in a week. Evolution is necessary. Needless to say, he lost his religious belief during the journey. The remainder of his life was spent in seclusion with his large family. He became and remained sickly and could work only two hours per day. Despite that he managed to create one of the most influential books of the nineteenth century: *On the Origin of Species* which described his 'Theory of Evolution', which broke with the old conception of a world created by God. It is hard to imagine now how shocking his book was in 1864. In it, he observed himself as sharply as he observed the natural world:

> I have said that in one respect my mind has changed during the last twenty years. Now for many years I cannot endure to read a line of poetry. I have also almost lost any taste for pictures and music. This curious and lamentable loss of a higher aesthetic taste is all the odder, as books on history, biographies and travels interests me as much as it ever did. My mind seems to have become a kind of machine for grinding general laws out of large collections of facts, but why this should have caused an atrophy of that part of the brain alone, on which higher tastes depend, I cannot conceive. The loss of these tastes is a loss of happiness and may possibly be injurious to the intellect and more probably to the moral character, by enfeebling the emotional part of our nature. (Darwin 1864)

What was Darwin's relation to genetics? He lived at the same time as Gregor Mendel, a monk who was the first to recognize the genetic laws governing inheritance of characteristics, but never came across Mendel's work. He also struggled with the laws of heredity and assumed that acquired characteristics could be inherited. Those opinions of Darwin's are largely forgotten; they do not gel with modern genetic thinking. Darwin's sharp self-observation shows that more is at work than just heredity in a human life. He was aware of the loss in his soul. He remarked somewhere that, if he could live again, he would take care to listen weekly to music and poetry. But are we not all in danger of losing our higher aesthetic senses? The capacity for the enjoyment of music must be nurtured. We pay attention to this in our schooling – pupils learn to appreciate classical music. Becoming open to classical music demands inner activity. Similar activity is needed if we are to be able to perceive the intact human being behind a syndrome. This ability fades if not actively practised.

Celtic cross slab, 7th or 8th century from Iona, Argyll, Scotland.

How can we meet the person behind a syndrome? The symbol of the cross can be of help. Grünewald's altarpiece reveals a magnificent Resurrection, but the suffering which preceded it was and is a real challenge. I grew up in the Catholic part of Holland and the image of the crucified Christ was everywhere. It was even next to our house, and, in my memory, more than life size. The drops of blood dripping down his chest were repainted regularly. On Good Fridays we went to church and followed the thirteen 'Stations of the Cross', depicting the events leading to the Crucifixion. Christ succumbs three times under the weight of the Cross, but three times recovers. The Catholic education, rich in colourful images, was a blessing to me and is now a source of strength. Once, in the yearly procession, I was even an angel – how heavy those wings were! I meet with different images of the Cross in Scotland. On the west coast a different mood is tangible. Traces can still be found of the Celtic Christian tradition. While there, I was struck by the hidden virtue and meaning of the Celtic Cross; this does not portray Christ with his head hanging down but is all movement, a streaming of lines. In the centre, these lines converge to create a space from which something like a sun begins to radiate. All this is held within the strict form of the Cross. Seeing this, I felt freed from the oppressive image of the hanging Christ.

In the Celtic Cross, resurrection seems to be the central theme, expressed by its radiant quality. Death and resurrection are united. To observe a Sun Cross creates a feeling of harmony. This process of encountering can happen where the vertical beam and the horizontal beam of the Cross meet. Similarly in our lives: we can imagine the horizontal stream to be our hereditary stream, the environment and family where we grow up. The vertical stream could represent our individuality which tries to relate to those realities. Most of us somehow manage this, to make our hereditary stream our own, and something starts to radiate.

This process of transformation is more difficult for a person with a genetic syndrome. The horizontal, hereditary stream is more determining, limits freedom; the individuality expressed in the vertical stream finds it difficult to transform the hereditary stream. This was demonstrated very obviously in the chapters in this book on the

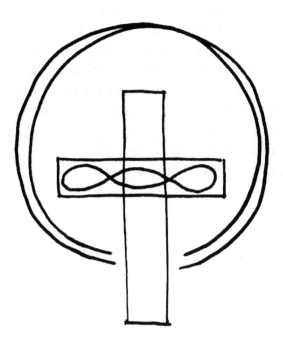

The Cross

various syndromes. Sometimes it can even happen that the genetic abnormalities are so strong that no real encounter can happen, and the
vertical cross turns inside out (see drawing). The sun starts to radiate
even more, the person himself is hardly visible but his presence can be
found in the environment, as we saw in Ronald's story in Chapter 13.

A cross to bear

2 February: Candlemas Day, the Feast of the Purification of the Virgin
Mary. It is a clear frosty night without wind. We collect our left-over
Christmas candles, but this year we don't melt them down as usual,
but place them in the garden. Next to our house is a memorial garden
with buried urns. Roses are planted in the form of a cross. Full of
enthusiasm, the children plant the candle stumps in the dark earth.
Suddenly, the black earth and the thorny rose bushes are transformed
into a radiating candle cross. Later the same evening, I walk with my

children through the dark night and show my oldest the star constellation called Orion. It stands brightly in a winter sky. 'Look,' exclaims the youngest, 'the stars are candles!' Suddenly I see it. The candle cross appears to be lifted up to heaven and all the lights have spread out. The barren cross was humanized by the candlelight; the heavens accepted it and it seems that the humanized suffering radiates back on us, supporting and strengthening. The Sun Cross: Good Friday and Easter morning are united in this image. Each of us can walk this path, independent of our genetic structure.

Bibliography

Ani, C., Grantham-McGregor, S. and Muller, D. (2000) 'Nutritional supplementation in Down Syndrome: Theoretical considerations and current status.' *Developmental Medicine & Child Neurology 42*, 207–213.

von Arnim, G. and Engel, P. (1964) 'Mental retardation related to hypercalcaemia.' *Developmental Medical Child Neurology 6*, 366–377.

Bauer, D. (1986) *Gespräche mit Ungeborenen: Kinder kündigen sich an.* ['Children Announce Themselves.'] Freies Geistesleben.

Beattie, J.O. (1992) 'Alcohol exposure and the fetus.' *European Journal of Clinical Nutrition 46*, 7–17.

Benda, C.E. (1947) *Mongolism and Cretinism.* London: William Heinemann.

Benda, C.E. (1960) *The Child with Mongolism: Congenital Acromicria.* New York: Grune and Stratton.

Bernhardt, B.A. (1997) 'Empirical evidence that genetic counseling is directive.' *American Journal for Human Genetics, 60*, 1, 17–21.

van Bos, W. (1997) 'Praags leven van strijd.' *Weekeditie nrc-Handelsblad,* 17 June.

Boston, S. (1994) *Too Deep for Tears.* London: Pandora.

Connor, M. and Ferguson-Smith, M. (1997) *Essential Medical Genetics.* Oxford: Blackwell Science.

Croockshank, F.G. (1931) *The Mongol in our Midst.* London: Kegan Paul, Trench, Trubner & Company.

Darwin, C. (1958) *The Autobiography of Charles Darwin, 1809–1882.* London: Collins.

Dawkins, R. (1976) *The Selfish Gene.* Oxford: Oxford University Press.

Denger, J. (1990) *Playdoyer für das Leben Mongoloide Kinder.* Stuttgart: Verlag Freies Geistesleben.

Dorris, M. (1992) *The Broken Cord. A Father's Story.* Warner Brooks.

Down, J.L. (1990) *Mental Affections of Childhood and Youth.* Oxford: Blackwell.

van Eeden, F. (1983) 'When our child smiled.' In *Spreuken, gedichten en liedjes voor kinderen.* Zeist: Christofoor. (Translated by the author.)

Fisher, E.P. (1991) *Die Beweglichkeit der Gene.* Scientific Publications Ltd. Goldmann Verlag.

Foudraine, J. (1971) *Wie is van Hout?* Ambo.

Fried, R. (1996) *Journal for Curative Education and Social Therapy,* Christmas/New Year.

Gershom, Y. (1992) *Beyond the Ashes.* Virginia: ARE Press.

Gold, L. (1996) *Cats are not Peas: A Calico History of Genetics.* New York: Springer Verlag.

Grünewald, P. (1997) *Journal for Curative Education and Social Therapy,* Summer, 1.

Hamer, D. and Copeland, P. (1998) *Living with our Genes.* London: Pan Books.

Harris, J.C. (1995) *Developmental Neuropsychiatry II.* Oxford: Oxford University Press.

Heaf, D. (2000) 'The human being.' *New View,* Autumn, 7–12.

Holdregde, G. (1996) *A Question of Genes. Understanding Life in Context.* Edinburgh: Floris Books.

Hubbard, R. and Wald, E. (1997) *Exploding the Gene Myth.* Boston, MA: Beacon Press.

Jones, K.L. (1997) *Smith's Recognisable Patterns of Human Malformations.* Philadelphia: W.B. Sanders Company.

Jones, S. (1997) *In the Blood: God, Genes and Destiny.* London: Flamingo.

Jordan, R. (1999) *Autistic Spectrum Disorders.* London: David Fulton Publishers.

Kent, T.K. (1946) *Materia Medica.* Philadelphia: Boericke & Tafel.

König, K. (1959) *Der Mongolismus.* Stuttgart: Hippokrates Verlag.

Lane, D. (1985) *Current Approaches to Down's Syndrome.* London: Holt, Rinehart and Winston.

Mae-Wan, H. (1997) *Genetic Engineering.* Bath: Gateway Books.

Mallalieu, B. (1997) 'x-certificate Behaviour.' *Guardian,* 12 June.

Mandela, N. (1994) *The Long Walk to Freedom.* Little Brown.

Müller-Wiedemann, H. (1996) *Karl König, a Central-European Biography of the Twentieth Century.* Camphill Books.

Nelkin, D. and Lindee, S. (1995) *The DNA Mystique: The Gene as a Cultural Icon.* New York: W.F. Freeman.

Niemeyer, M.H., Gast Kemper, M. and Kamps, F.H.M. (1999) *Ontwikkelings Stoornissen bij Kinderen.* Assen: Van Gorcum.

O'Brien, G. and Yule, W. (1995) *Behavioral Phenotypes.* Cambridge: MacKeith Press.

Phethean, R. (1998) *Journal for Curative Education and Social Therapy,* Summer, 4–13.

Ridley, M. (1999) *Genome.* London: Fourth Estate.

Sacks, O. (1996) *The Island of the Colour Blind.* Picador.

Sahlman, L., Weihs, A. and Ureki, B. (1996) *The Higher Senses and the Seven Life Proceesses.* Camphill Books.

Shapiro, B.L. (1994) 'The environmental basis of the Down Syndrome phenotype.' *Developmental Medicine and Child Neurology 36,* 84–90.

Silvers, R. (1997) *Hidden Histories of Science.* London: Granta Books.

Sinason, V. (1992) *Mental Handicap and the Human Condition.* London: Free Association Books.

Steiner, R. (1980) *Voeding en Bewustzijn.* Zeist: Vrij Geestesleven.

Steiner, R. (1998) *Education for Special Needs.* London: Rudolf Steiner Press.

Steinhausen, H.C., Willms, J. and Spohr, H-L. (1993) 'Long-term psychopathological and cognitive outcome of children with Fetal Alcohol Syndrome.' *Journal of the American Academy of Child and Adolescent Psychiatry 32,* 5, 990–994.

Stratford, B. (1989) *Down's Syndrome.* Harmondsworth: Penguin Books.

Stressguth, A.P. *et al.* (1991) 'Fetal Alcohol Syndrome in adolescents and adults.' *Journal of the American Medical Association 265,* 15 (1961–1967).

Travers, P.L. (1994) *Mary Poppins in the Park.* London: Lions.

Trevarthen, C., Aitken, K.J., Papoudi, D. and Robarts, J.Z. (1998) *Children with Autism: Diagnosis and Interventions to Meet their Needs.* London: Jessica Kingsley Publishers.

Watson, J.D. (1968) *The Double Helix. A Personal Account of the Discovery of the Structure of DNA.* London: Weidenfeld and Nicolson.

Weihs, T.J. (2000) *Children in Need of Special Care.* Revised edition. London: Souvenir Press.

Williams, J.C.P., Barratt-Boyes, B.G., and Lowe, J.B. (1961) 'Supravalvular aortic stenosis.' *Circulation 24,* 1311–1318.

Williams, Angelman, H. *et al.* (1995) 'Angelman Syndrome: Consensus for diagnostic criteria.' *American Journal of Medical Genetics 56.*

Wirz, J. (1997) *The Future of DNA.* Dordrecht: Kluwert Academic Publisher.

Wirz, J. (1996) 'Schritte zur Komplementarität in der Genetik.' *Elemente der Naturwissenschaft 96.*

Subject Index

Author Index